To my mother-in-law, Marion Ducey Norton (1898 – 1993).
Truly my best friend, we stepped onto this path together
and walked the early steps of the journey, arm in arm.

- LaVrene

To my mother-in-law Joyce Meyer (1930 – 2006)
whose courage and faith showed us
how to leave this life and embrace the next.

- Steve

Supported by the Sunflower Foundation of Topeka, Kansas; the Kansas Department on Aging, and The Commonwealth Fund (a national, private foundation based in New York City that supports independent research on health and social issues.) The views presented here are those of the author and not necessarily those of the funders, its directors, officers or staff.

Disclaimer
This publication is designed to provide information in regard to the subject matter covered. and is sold with the understanding that the publisher and authors are not rendering professional advice and are not responsible for decisions and actions taken by users of the publication.

ISBN-10: 0-9793682-0-0
ISBN-13: 978-09793682-0-2

Design by Kristine Kamikawa

Action Pact Press

table of contents

As With Sunbeam

The pursuit of happiness has been recognized as central to our humanity for centuries. We put endless effort into the pursuit. Whether it's pleasure or pain – it's part of the hunt. We experience it as a momentary satisfaction when we find the perfect gift for a loved one or enjoy a cup of coffee with a friend. It erupts with deeper meaning in moments of family unity with a group hug or when we turn to a neighbor at worship with the sign of peace. We experience pain when we push through the hard things to achieve happiness - going to work day after day, saving dollars with our children to contribute to those less fortunate. The drive and the satisfaction are in the hunt. What if you couldn't pursue happiness? What if you were no longer in charge?

"The rights of mankind are not to be rummaged for among old parchments or musty records. They are written, as with sunbeam in the whole volume of human nature, by the hand of Divinity itself, and can never be erased or obscured by mortal power." - Alexander Hamilton

The words "life, liberty and the pursuit of happiness" ring true for everyone in America, but they fall flat for the frail living in institutional care. They are rights not granted or created but, centuries ago, secured by the Declaration of Independence as rights our forefathers considered inherent in each American. So, how is it we assume our elders hand over these rights as they cross the threshold into a nursing home?

Certainly elders are not slaves or prisoners, yet many freedoms we take for granted now elude them. No choice in surroundings, what and when to eat, when and how to bathe, when to go to bed or when to rise. No privacy upon desire, no freedom to leave, and worse – alarms that frighten when getting up from a chair or bed. No choice in how to spend one's time. Meaning and purpose ignored and rarely nurtured.

Let's acknowledge the pursuit as central to who we are as human beings. Let's assure choice in the daily lives of elders and in our own future as pertinent to the pursuit. Written as with sunbeam by the hand of Divinity itself, these rights cannot be guaranteed in a parchment or in the pages if this book, but must be acted upon by all to assure our humanity.

Foreword

The Household Model

This book and the accompanying materials are for everyone who serves in long-term care and wants a rich, meaningful life for residents and fulfillment in their work.

It is for you, the leaders and providers of nursing home services; nurses, board members, aides, shareholders, housekeepers, administrators, cooks, social workers, owners and activity professionals. It is for all who dread the thought of living in today's conventional nursing facility and dream of a real home for the frail and elderly.

This book is not for people who seek a gradualist approach to change. It is for those who want a revolutionary transformation in the culture of nursing homes and other long-term care settings. The transformation we advocate calls for a new framework and operating principles that make the old ways obsolete.

It's about creating a new foundation for long-term care: Home versus institution, person over system, self-determination and shared decision-making rather than subordination. It is about transforming everything we do, how we do it and how we relate to everyone including ourselves.

It is about making the move to a long-term care facility a simple change of address rather than the loss of home, purpose and identity. It is about making the nursing home a place for living rather than for waiting to die--a vision impossible to fulfill within the current framework of care.

Within this collection of observations, stories and guidelines, we try to establish a new framework for creating, with elders, what we *all* recognize as home; that place where we find sanctuary and a deep sense of wellbeing; where people live, work and self-actualize together.

We, the authors, have committed our lives to replacing the institutional culture and its environmental trappings with surroundings that foster warm, personal relationships; where small groups of elders--supported by self-led teams of employees--determine their own lives and build community. We call it the "Household Model."

Though it is a revolutionary departure from the status quo, it still is less than what our elders and their caregivers truly deserve. Until broader society reexamines its beliefs and values about old age and reshapes itself accordingly, the Household Model is simply a bridge on the long road to a rich and fulfilling elderhood.

Charting a Highway to Home

Revolutionary change always begins with a small group of committed people. They are pioneers who enjoy the exhilaration of discovery, for which they also suffer and take calculated risks. They stumble and fall, then get back on their feet and forge ahead.

Pioneers blaze trails for others to follow and improve upon. The first path is never the straightest or quickest, but it makes the journey easier for those who follow. Each subsequent traveler makes the path a bit smoother for the next.

The Lewis and Clark Expedition suffered untold hardship and uncertainty while exploring the uncharted western frontiers of 19th Century America. Their legacy is their map, followed by thousands of pioneers who laid deep ruts in the earth with their wagon trains. Outposts cropped up along the way, providing sustenance and critical information for weary travelers. Though their journeys were generally easier than Lewis and Clark's, they too endured incredible hardship.

Wagon ruts evolved into dirt roads, pavement and, ultimately, an interstate highway system lined with services for travelers' every comfort. We give little thought to the struggles of Lewis and Clark as we cruise in our luxury vehicles along precision-engineered, six-lane highways. Yet their sacrifice and commitment precede everything interstate travelers take so much for granted today.

This book and the accompanying *Household Matters – A Good Life 'Round the Clock* kit are intended as early outposts along the wagon trail leading to a real home for long-term care residents. It is based on trail blazing by earlier explorers bent on changing the culture of long-term care.

No doubt you may encounter bumps we did not anticipate in the path we've laid out. Each new journey has its own perils and rewards. But we believe this offering will lead you around many treacherous pitfalls to more rewards than you thought possible. You, in turn, will make the path smoother for those who follow.

Only after more of us begin the journey will it become a major thoroughfare to a better life for elders and caregivers – a highway to home.

Mindset for Reading: Search for Meaning and Purpose

By reading this book you are exercising just one of the many ways we seek meaning and purpose in life. Our interactions and relationships with friends and family, our hobbies, spiritual endeavors, work, hunger to learn and pursuit of happiness are all part of the search. How we seek and what we find becomes our legacy.

In the book, *The Art of Happiness at Work*, the Dalai Lama and Howard C. Cutler, M.D., conclude there are three focuses in doing our work: survival, career and calling. Survival is the focus that provides us with money for food, shelter and clothing. Career focuses on advancement in our trade and society. But calling, they find, is the focus that most impacts our level of satisfaction with our work. Calling is the great meaning and purpose of life.

If we try, we can find meaning and purpose in just about any job. It may be indirect or on a small scale, but we can find it. However, few jobs hold as much profound opportunity for finding it as eldercare, where the work itself gives meaning and purpose to the everyday lives of frail elders. It's a beautiful interdependency: in giving we receive the very gift we impart.

We know that meaning and purpose are very personal. They are not something someone can hand us in a nice package. They are what drive us from deep inside. They may feel like intellectual concepts or emotions, but in fact they are also actions. They are potential fulfilled. They do not sit and wait. If we heed their voice, they drive us. They are our identity.

Knowing this, we see we cannot live out for elders the meaning and purpose in their lives, or place those fulfillments gently in their laps. We must, however, create a climate in which they, themselves, can explore, develop and live out their own pursuits.

The importance of meaning and purpose in life is one reason the culture change movement was born in the late 1990s. Returning to elders the right to direct their own lives is not a mere change of regulation or procedure. It's not just steps to take as directed by a prescriptive manual. It is a change of culture. It is a new context. Because the nursing home industry has been procedure-driven for so long, many fail to fully understand that changes in context and culture must precede and accompany procedural changes.

The new cultural mindset sees elders for who they are and who they can be. The old one sees them for who they are not. The new mindset not only birthed the culture change movement, it led it to the Household Model.

The Household Model graduates beyond leaving behind

the institution by replacing it with true home. It nurtures human relationships and builds community. It strives for the normalcy of daily life that we all recognize while providing strong clinical care and other services needed by the elderly and frail. Let these ideals be your companions on your personal and organizational journey.

Household Matters – A Good Life 'Round the Clock

This book is intended as a context and umbrella for the accompanying *Household Matters* kit. The components of the kit are designed to satisfy some of the hunger for "how to" information you may feel during the painful unlearning and relearning necessary for your vision of change to take root. In addition to this book, the *Household Matters* kit includes:

(1) Daybreak – Creating Home: Policies and Procedures

(2) Midday – Living and Working in Harmony: Integrated Human Resource System

(3) Evensong – Reflecting on Quality: A Quality Process and Measurement System

There may be a natural tendency to pull out pieces of this kit and use them for a specific change you desire in your progression to the Household Model. We strongly encourage that. But first we suggest you read the book in its entirety, and then work through the rest of the kit components until you have a whole view of the context and its parts. This allows you to discern and carefully select the pieces that work for you, and then set them in motion. It also better equips you, as a change agent in your organization, to lead, influence and design your own journey.

Icons note sections that inspire action.

 "Try This" icons suggest exercises.

 "Think About It" icons notate opportunity for reflection.

 "Living and Working in Harmony" icons refer you to the team training guide for further study and exercises.

Once you have read the book and reviewed the accompanying kit systems, you can use them in many ways. We offer the following examples:

• Select a chapter that speaks to an issue you currently face and read through it.

- Scan highlighted quotes in the margins to refresh your memory and awaken thoughts.
- Seek out the stories contained within, then read all around the story to understand the full context.
- Search for answers when you're perplexed at a snag in your journey.
- Pick out a "Think About It" or "Try This" exercise.
- Tie book chapters and subtopics to other contents of the Household Matters kit for study.
- E-mail the authors and have a follow-up dialogue.
- Pull out pieces to assist with designing and implementing a specific change project.
- Create your own master action plan with components of the *Household Matters* kit assigned to specific action teams to complete.

Finally, give meaning and purpose to your journey by sharing stories as we have within these pages. Stories personalize and bring to life the dry data of everyday struggle. They inspire, comfort and support us when we are down. They immortalize lessons learned from both victory and defeat. Stories heal.

Our ancient ancestors wove the fabric of culture and community through storytelling around the campfire. As if clearing a path for the next generation, stories from centuries ago instruct today's children about values and principles for meaningful living before they can read and write.

Let storytelling weave your new culture by routinely bringing together staff, residents and family members to freely share their experiences. Let the stories help clear the path for those who follow in your footsteps toward revolutionizing the lives of elders for decades to come.

chapter 1
The Way It Is

"I long, as does every human being, to be at home wherever I find myself."
- Maya Angelou

She screamed for years but nobody really heard it until she stopped. It was a shrill, penetrating, constant and unsettling shriek; a noise not readily identified as human. Words were not part of it. She could not form them. Instead, it was like the cry of a trapped and desperate animal hoping someone could hear and understand. The howl haunted the nursing home corridors like a shackled ghost intent on settling its business, belying that the source of the sound was less than five feet tall, not even 90 pounds, and unable to walk.

Her Asian skin was healthy and beautiful. The Meadowlark Hills staff moistened it with lotion, turned her at night and repositioned her at specified intervals. Lee Chung Hi lived year after year, perched in a reclining Geri-chair. It kept her safe and in place. Her graying black hair was brushed and shining. Vital signs were monitored with regularity and her care-plan was carefully executed. She was bathed on schedule at three o'clock on Tuesday and Friday afternoons. By all valued and applied measures in long-term care, she was well cared for. In the nursing notes, and in the minds of all who cared for her, the never-ending screams were the result of dementia…an illness of the mind, which surely must have caused her initial placement. But then, nobody remembered for sure.

The other residents were routinely lined up outside the dining room to wait for lunch. Lee Chung Hi ate alone in her chair, parked in the corridor farthest from where people gathered. Nobody – resident, staff or visitor – wanted to be near her. Caregivers attended to her dutifully, yet her noise repelled them. She ate alone, sat alone and slept alone.

She became her noise in the eyes of everyone. But nobody could hear her screaming for what it *truly* was. It never occurred to us that *we* might be the cause of it - we, who carry out the biddings of a system lethal to the human spirit.

Years passed before we finally understood it. And not until we transformed Meadowlark Hills into a vibrant household community and witnessed Lee Chung Hi's parallel transformation did we realize how profoundly appropriate her screaming had been in response to the dehumanizing conditions in which she lived.

It was as if her shrieks channeled the despair of millions of elders trapped within the lifeless culture of today's conventional nursing homes. It seems that nearly every family in America has its own personal story of grief born out of their nursing home experiences. But for the most part, the realization the system *must* change eludes society.

How Should Society's Elders Live?

We believe that elders, no matter how frail, should enjoy the comforts and security of home wherever they reside. Like anyone else, they have the right to determine the framework of their own individual lives and where they fit in their community. They should enjoy spontaneity, choice in how to spend their days, the reciprocity of relationships that bring purpose and meaning to their lives and a place to call home.

Unfortunately, today's typical nursing home provides just the opposite. It is so unnatural at its very core, mere improvements in the current system fall drastically short of nurturing good health, wholesome living, rich community life and the potential for self-actualization.

The current system betrays not only our elders, but also the compassion and spirit of service that call caregivers to their profession. It is enough to make anyone scream.

We Know Them

Nobody intended it to be this way – a national system of warehouses for the old and frail served by otherwise caring staff who are reduced to performing like assembly-line workers. After all, the people who live in nursing homes are our parents, relatives, friends, neighbors and former colleagues. We know them.

They gave us life, enrolled us in school and tried to buy us the perfect birthday gift. They counseled, encouraged and admonished us when we needed it.

They served in government, fought wars and put out fires. They built our roads, schools and hospitals. They did what was asked and needed of them. When one-by-one they grew old, they passed responsibility for the world to us, one-by-one in a timeless, perpetual ritual. As they passed the baton, each in his or her way wished us well, hoping we would do better. In return, we owe them more than they are getting.

One day, sooner than we think, we will become the elders and pass the baton to our children. When that day comes, what will the long-term-care system offer us?

A Paradox

We have a tragic paradox here: A dehumanizing, regimented and often cruel system created piecemeal by thousands of people over a span of decades has been inherited and perpetuated by very decent, heart-

"The current system betrays not only our elders, but also the compassion and spirit of service that call caregivers to their profession."

filled people who love elders.

It is a dilemma for us, the inheritors, because to be true to our hearts we must admit we work in a failed enterprise. It is difficult to hear we have given our lives to something fundamentally flawed because we personalize it and hear that *we* are flawed. Then we may become defensive and refuse to hear the real message. This isn't about us being flawed. It's about good people working in a deeply flawed system.

We must not let that confuse us.

Most of us have a calling to the care-giving profession—perhaps prodded since childhood by the memory of a beloved grandparent or family friend—or we would not be in it. The problem is that the daily tasks our job requires do not fulfill the spirit of our calling.

Yet we continue down the same dismal path because, beyond personal defensiveness and rationalizations, we are loyal to our organizations. We defend how we collectively do things. We become so indoctrinated by rigid systems that we believe it necessary to do things the way we do. We don't let ourselves confront our own beliefs.

We learn to adapt. We let the compassionate inner voice that directed us to this work recede beneath the din of schooling, job training, timetables and tightly monitored routines until, God forbid, some of us quit hearing it all together. Yet we truly believe we are doing what we are *supposed* to do. After all, those of us who directly serve residents are measured every day by how efficiently we complete our assignments.

Top Down Hierarchy Creates Silos of Self-Interest

"A broken system has been inherited and perpetuated by very decent, heart-filled people who love elders."

Most of us who manage long-term care organizations believe we must be structured hierarchically and reserve judgment and decision-making for those at the top. Workers without formal power are managed by systems that rob residents, family members and those directly serving them of the opportunity to make timely decisions affecting the most basic aspects of everyday life.

"We're taught to believe that those who provide direct service must be managed through policies, protocols, tightly designed routines and quality improvement outcome measuring."

The Administrator and Director of Nursing are universally acknowledged as the most powerful of brokers. In addition, we place a slew of middle managers--reinforced by assistant managers and supervisors—in charge of each area and function to ensure those assigned to them do what is supposed to be done when it is supposed to be done. Departmentalized silos typically arise as a result, with individual departments competing with one another and becoming isolated from the broader purpose of service.

We apparently don't believe caregivers possess the judgment required to make decisions within their own realms. So, we manage them through inflexible policies, protocols, regimented scheduling and quality improvement measurements, which they learn to adhere to in place of their own good judgment.

Put bluntly, "we" don't think "they" can do it. We're wrong. Across the country a growing number of progressive companies are being liberated by decentralized power and decision-making. It works, whereas, if we take stock of the past and present, it is obvious that reserved and centralized power hasn't done much for us.

Task Trumps Individual Needs

What truly is important of course, are the people in an organization. But we don't measure the value of meeting individual needs that otherwise collide with the daily regime. Nurse aides, for example, quickly learn an important measure of their work is whether routines are completed on time, like waking up residents in succession in seven-minute increments so everyone gets to breakfast within an hour. The aide is not evaluated on how residents are affected when pulled out of sweet dreams at 5:47 a.m. No one takes stock of the compassion and fellowship suppressed beneath the frantic rush to meet protocol. Rather, the measure is whether the job is completed on time. The aide's incentive is to depersonalize residents by reducing each to a seven-minute task.

We never bother to consider following individualized schedules so each resident can awaken naturally and pursue his or her own special interests throughout the day. If we caught an aide relaxing in an easy chair with a resident, holding hands and watching *Days of Our Lives*, she would be written up and counseled. We're too busy with assigned tasks like creating an MDS or charting progress notes. The artificial rush we manufacture with schedules and protocols is an affront to what is a truly productive way of caring for human beings.

Nurse aides tell us they literally have to turn off a switch in their heads and dismiss the humanity of the resident they are serving before they can complete their wakeup routines on time to avoid the backlash that would come from management for taking proper time with each person.

We can't fathom organizing ourselves around the premise that each resident has the right to make *all* their own daily life decisions like when to arise, when and what to eat, when and how to be bathed and what to do for the rest of the day. So we resist or minimize the enormity of it by making little changes (get a dog, organize a buffet or bring in plants) without changing the context of the organizational structure, values and operating systems.

The Nursing Home System Is Broken

Today's typical nursing home is crafted on the inherently divisive notion of "us" and "them." Deeply rooted ageism in society combined with an Industrial Age assembly line mentality have led "us" middle aged adults to create a system of dealing with "them," the alumni of active adulthood now turned frail and old. We seem to forget we feel about the same in our skin as we did when we were much younger, and that we will still feel much the same when we are old.

While our material needs change at different stages in our life, we are still the same person through childhood, adulthood and elderhood. We lose sense of that when designing the system for "them." Consequently, we put the system's perceived efficiencies ahead of what is best for the individual.

"We" become "them" with each passing of the baton of responsibility from frail elder to active adult, so in reality the nursing homes we create are ultimately for us. We would never purposely design a nursing home system like we have if we imagine ourselves in its care, where:

- We are viewed as a diagnosis rather than as a person.
- We are served within a militaristic organizational structure that values pursuit of task over warmth of human contact.
- We are housed in a depersonalized physical environment where the only choice in shared quarters is a bed near the window or one next to the bathroom.
- Privacy is found only by retreating into slumping and slumber.

That is just the beginning of a long list of indignities endured throughout the day, every day by nursing home residents in nearly every town in the nation. The trickle of systems-driven dehumanization has turned into a flood that is drowning our elders and their family members and eventually will engulf us as well.

"We would never purposely design a nursing home system like we have if we imagine ourselves in its care."

Widgets and Warehouses – Industrial Age Thinking

Imagine the assembling of widgets as they proceed from one worker to the next along a factory assembly line, and you will see a strong relationship to the traditional nursing home model in America. The first worker attaches an electronic board, the next adds a spring, the third a switch, a fourth encases it all in a plastic shell and a fifth packages the widgets four to a box, 20 boxes to a case and stacks them into neat rows in a warehouse to await shipping to their final destinations.

Assembly line workers concentrate on their singular tasks. They rarely see the finished product and need not understand how their jobs relate to the whole. Employees work quickly to avoid falling behind and incurring the wrath of fellow workers up and down the line.

Supervisors and quality control experts clutching clipboards scurry about in a very businesslike manner. Forklifts and carts with flashing lights and beepers weave their way around busy workstations, machinery and factory room accessories. The physical plant, stark in appearance, is designed not for aesthetics but to maximize worker efficiency and widget output. The aroma of industrial solvents and lubricants hangs in the air.

Now imagine yourself in the typical T-shaped nursing home. Nurse aides rush from resident to resident, waking, toileting and bathing them. Nurses do assessments, pass out medications and attend to immediate needs. Dietary workers prepare scores of identical food trays in assembly line fashion. All individual tasks conform to the demands of a rigid and regimented system. Heaven help the worker who falls behind schedule.

Got a spill? Call housekeeping. Resident needs a pad change? Alert a nurse aide. Like widgets, residents by day's end have been hurriedly picked over by dozens of hands, each pair trained primarily for a specific task.

The physical environment is more akin to an office building or hospital than a home. Titanic nurses' stations guard entry to long, shiny tiled hallways illuminated by fluorescent lights and littered with med carts, mechanical lifts, wheelchairs, trash cans and dirty linen bins. Intercoms intrude on private thoughts. Call lights flash and beep. Metal carts go clickity-clack down hallways. The odor of disinfectant mixed with urine greets all who enter.

Residents share identical, uninspiring bedrooms lined up on either side of bustling hallways through which the whole world passes. Intimate conversations between family members are separated from roommates in cramped quarters by only a thin curtain. Few if any of the residents'

"Imagine the assembling of widgets as they proceed from one worker to the next along a factory assembly line and you will see the strong relationship to the traditional nursing model in America."

personal items adorn the walls or nightstand.

A herd-like mentality presides, with residents lined up to await entry to the dining hall and moved en masse to bingo games and other group activities. Much of the residents' day is spent parked near the nurses' stations or in other public spaces as if waiting to be shipped to their final destination.

What If It Were You?

Imagine *your* life lived in the public eye, sharing a semi-private room where your roommate's family comes in and crowds around his or her bed, trying in vain not to intrude on your turf. Chances are they are as uncomfortable as you are. Forced together like strangers in an elevator, you turn aside to avoid eye contact.

Hundreds of people walk by your bedroom door each day, often looking in as they brisk by. Your only escape from prying eyes is a small area in the corner of your room beyond their visual span. Your bedroom, shared with somebody you have never met prior to being admitted, is often entered by staff without knocking. Or, they knock and walk in without stopping to wait for your invitation to enter.

Throughout the nursing home, you relinquish control to authority figures. From the moment you are awakened until you are put to bed, they shuffle you from one situation or place to another within the confines of the day's schedule. Any resistance by you is met with patronizing but kind attempts to keep you in the flow. You pity the caregiver for her workload when she tells you they are short staffed. You fear your objections hold her up in her rush to meet schedule, so eventually you quit asserting yourself.

We must learn to see ourselves in the faces of elders if we are to cultivate the empathy needed to create a real home with them. Imagine yourself as a resident. What if it were *you*?

The System: Ill-Conceived From the Start

A textbook would provide a detailed and referenced account of the history of nursing homes, how they were started and where they went wrong. But this is not a textbook or technical paper. It is a guide to change. There already are texts on nursing home history, and most agree something went awry.

The traditional nursing home model was ill conceived from the

"We must learn to see ourselves in the faces of elders if we are to cultivate the empathy needed to create a real home with them."

start, yet we keep adding bandages year after year hoping to improve it. In addition, the federal government continues to increase regulatory oversight while simultaneously cutting reimbursement for services that already is below the cost of providing them. As they have for years, they demand more for less because they have the power to do so.

The result is a broken system. Even some of the most prominent industry leaders agree the system does not work, though some act as if it were only recently broken.

In an open letter to the President of the United States, Larry Minnix, President of the American Association of Homes and Services for the Aging says, "The transition from today's broken long-term care system to a new era of consumer centered care cannot morally be paved with a cutback, make-do, rationing strategy on the backs of the Greatest Generation – whose efforts brought us the freedom and prosperity we enjoy today."

This book is not about improving nursing homes. It is about overcoming them. When the foundation of a house is rotten, you don't waste time and resources by painting the porch. You rebuild. You start over. It's a fundamental principle.

We keep painting the porch and patching the roof of a failed system by investing in symptom correction. We don't get to the root causes. We treat interrelated issues like workforce turnover and clinical outcomes as isolated problems. We try to fix them with recycled programs on staff recruitment, education and retention, clinical protocols and measurements; the list goes on. But few people at the funding or policy level have identified the root of the problem and set out to change it.

The framework of the nursing home system itself must be replaced. Bad framework produces bad outcomes that can't be fixed by throwing money and education at the inevitable symptoms. Government and foundations spend millions every year on workforce development and clinical improvement programs. Yet cycle after cycle, turnover rates aren't reduced and outcomes do not significantly improve. In its December 2005 Report to Congressional Requesters on Nursing Homes, the Government Accountability Office told Congress the current approach is not working. But as with other similar diagnoses, they did not satisfactorily articulate why. Like others before them, they poke at symptoms.

Perhaps they just didn't talk to the right people. According to Mickus, Luz and Hogan in their article, "Voices From the Front," nurse aides say they leave because they are not valued by the organization, they have too many residents and can't provide quality care, their pay is too low and

"This book is not about improving nursing homes. It's about overcoming them."

opportunities for job advancement are rare.

But we have not listened. Workforce programs may improve recruitment, but the cycle of turnover does not improve. At best it is a vicious cycle.

Employee turnover alone costs the industry $2.5 billion per year. Yet we don't think we can afford to change the system, according to Seavey in his article "The Cost of Frontline Turnover in LTC." If all the dollars spent chasing symptoms were aligned and redirected to creating a new framework for nursing homes, the transformation could dramatically improve the lives of elders and their caregivers now and for generations to come.

We can't afford, economically or morally, *not* to change the system. If we are to be true to our calling as care providers, we have a moral imperative to transform sterile, institutionalized nursing facilities into *real* homes where elders may live to their full potential to the end of their days. If we are to be true to ourselves as people, we are morally bound to overcome the present system. It is our future and our children's. And, if we can think beyond the next income statement or shareholders' report, we will understand that creating true homes for elders is good business. Giving customers what they truly want and deserve is always good business.

Not just providers, but everyone – policy-makers, regulators, communities and families – must change. We providers must lead the change. We're the ones entrusted with the system, and only we, with support from others, can lead the change.

We, the authors, travel the United States and beyond to help guide long-term care organizations through the struggle and exhilaration that come with transforming institutions into true homes. Between the two of us, we have been in every state in the union and seen countless nursing facilities. We have learned we can walk into any nursing home in America and describe, almost down to the minute, how they do things. We can describe where the difficult relationships between departments lie, joke about them to people who work there, and they laugh knowingly. We can do that within minutes after walking through their door for the first time, not because we are so smart, but because it is practically the same everywhere.

Some nursing homes have "hotelized" the lobby with chandeliers and nice furniture, but most still wake residents at the crack of dawn and, in assembly line fashion, pull them out of bed, clean, dress and set them into a wheelchair in the span of a few minutes. Many still line elders

"If all the dollars spent chasing symptoms were aligned and redirected to creating a new framework for nursing homes, the transformation could dramatically improve the lives of elders and their caregivers now and for generations to come."

"We have a moral imperative to transform sterile institutions into real homes."

"We providers must lead the change. We're the ones entrusted with the system, and only we, with support from others, can lead the change."

up at the dining hall. Once at the table they plop entrées shaped like ice-cream scoops onto plates under dusty rose insulated covers on plastic trays crowded with packaged condiments, liquid nutrients and medication Dixie cups. And they still park residents in half moon formations around the nurses' station where they sit slumped and dozing throughout the day because it's "where the action is."

Nobody wants to claim credit for the system as it now stands. In fact, if today's nursing home system were proposed as a new concept, it would be rejected as a bad idea. Still, there are a lot of people trying to hang on to it.

More and more care providers are trying earnestly to move on to something better, but they keep pulling the past into their vision of the future by building upon the current framework. We can't move forward unless we let go of what has failed us. We won't let go until we look it square in the eye with objective clarity and see it for what it is. Otherwise, we'll take too much of the old, failed system with us. At best, we'll improve it, but not overcome it.

People outside the long-term care industry have known all along the system is broken. That is why placing family members in nursing homes is so painful, and why so many elders say they would rather die than go to one. But only *now*, in the century after the system emerged, are we providers allowing ourselves to see how truly broken it is. In our hearts, we have known it all along. We just got indoctrinated and forgot.

"People outside the long-term care industry have known all along the system is broken."

chapter 2
Regulatory Impact on Change

*"For every thousand hacking at the leaves of evil
there is only one striking at the root."*
- Henry David Thoreau

My Nursing Home Experience - By Imogene Higbie, Age 87*

I entered the nursing home on a stretcher on Good Friday. The ambulance attendants wheeled me through the front door of the assisted living area. No one was in the office and the reception desk was unattended even though it was around 10:30 a.m. I later learned it was always like this on weekends and holidays.

After checking in at the nursing station, the driver took me to room 224 and placed me on my back on a flowered polyester bedspread covering a sagging mattress. The thin pillows were of little comfort. No staff person spoke to me when I rolled in. After a few minutes on the bed in my hospital clothes and shoes and with no cover, someone came in to say I could rest there until time for the mid-day meal in the dining room.

Although I could walk if assisted, I could not pull myself to a sitting position, turn on my side or get out of bed. So there I was, trapped in a strange place, weak, sick and totally dependent. I could not even reach the call button. I learned this was a common predicament.

As I waited I looked around and saw I had a roommate. She slept, attached to machines that surrounded her bed and made soft wheezing noises. I could see she must be extremely ill. I felt uneasy in the presence of a woman I did not know and who possibly was dying.

Around noon a sober-faced nurse came to take me to the dining room. Dressed only in my hospital bathrobe and shoes, I walked with her through the central hall and past the nursing station. I was surprised to see patients in rehabilitation sharing rooms with those who were chronically ill or suffering from dementia.

Near the nursing station, patients were parked against the walls, watching each other being given medications from a tiered cart. There was little interaction among them. Many made vocal sounds indicating dementia. My heart went out to them as I looked into their eyes while we slowly walked by.

The nurse seated me at a table opposite a glare of light from a large window with a beautiful view of the harbor. I had no appetite, so a kind CNA escorted me back to my room, opened the bed and helped me under the covers where I slept.

I had chosen to come here for rehabilitation therapy following radical surgery because of the facility's reputation as one of the best in the state. The 42-bed nursing home is attached to 24 assisted living units. I lived in the former for 15 days and the latter for six months.

Some of the assisted living residents called the nursing home "the other side" – a place no one wanted to be. Some never even wanted to visit friends there. Many of my friends who have gone through rehab in other nursing homes tell me one of the most important goals of their recovery was to "get out of that awful place."

Although I do not consider my nursing home an awful place, I certainly left there as soon as I possibly could. When I realized I was stuck there, I decided I would be cheerful and cooperative and cultivate a positive attitude. It helped, but I stumbled and faltered many times.

One reason was the lack of personal space and privacy. Originally designed for one occupant, our rooms were crowded with two patients and their beds, side tables and chairs; one dresser with only six small drawers and one closet. The lighting was poor, consistently either too dark or too bright and glaring.

Our "private" bathroom (toilet and wash basin) was big enough for a wheelchair, but sparsely furnished with a small cabinet, an inadequate number of towels and no washcloths. It supposedly was cleaned every other day but not well.

Patients who were mobile could escape their cramped quarters by venturing into the hallways or the large room surrounding the nursing station and staff offices (i.e., Control Central). The dining room was sometimes available, but staff often held meetings there. Patients who were wheelchair bound or afflicted with dementia were parked near the nursing station where they watched the activity, dozed and received medications from a med tech pushing a large cart.

My first nursing home bathing experience made me yearn for my warm shower at home. Two or three times a week each patient was taken to a colorless, chilly corner of a bathing room where there was hoisting equipment. There, I sat in a cold metal chair while tepid water was run over me. An attendant rubbed me with a washcloth and detergent, and then dried me with a thin towel as I shivered.

There appeared to be no controlling who walked through the nursing home. One night after 11 p.m., a man appeared at my bedside to take my blood pressure. I had never seen him before. He said he was from an outside agency because the assigned RN had not appeared. (There was obviously a high rate of staff turnover because even during the short time I was in the nursing home there were many new faces). I never saw the man again. When I inquired, no regular staff seemed to know him.

Another day a man appeared, saying he was my occupational

therapist (OT) and I should get up and meet with him. Since I already had an assigned OT, I refused. He told me my refusal would look really bad on my chart.

By the third day in the nursing home my usual defenses were no longer holding up and I was feeling pretty down. During the first two days I was able to reach my newspapers and began to adapt to the new routine, but there were times when my room was crowded with my roommate's polite but noisy relatives, separated from me by only a flimsy, white cloth curtain. When neither of our families was visiting, I was left alone with this silent woman.

I was told she was in a coma and expected to die soon. After supper while waiting to be put to bed I realized no one in her family would be with her that night if she died. I would be her only witness. I felt great sorrow for her aloneness and unnerved by my assigned, un-requested role in this second most important event in the woman's life – her death.

When the aide came to help me to bed I was hysterical. With the aide's help I went, crying, to the nursing station. After pouring out my story to Cindy, the RN on duty, I was calmer but could not stop crying. Cindy was at once empathic, human and marvelously professional. She called my daughters at my request. They came immediately and helped Cindy find a bed for me in another room.

The next morning I learned my roommate died during the night. A wave of guilt washed over me as I struggled with the feelings I had deserted a friend when she needed me.

As I write these remembrances I am surprised how angry I am at the system our country has created to house and care for old citizens. It is shamefully inadequate, joyless, bland – often even cruelly neglectful and abusive.

During my own experience I was dismayed by the lack of personal autonomy and involvement by residents in making decisions about their personal lives, and the pervasive assumption staff knew what was best for us better than we knew for ourselves.

Although the caregivers in assisted living and nursing homes are almost always people of good will and kindly intent, they, too, are trapped in a destructive, stultifying and exceedingly complex system that, bound by government regulations and corporate greed, is seemingly impervious to change.

I am angry. I want a better life for my peers and myself. I have a passionate wish that our children will enjoy a happier and more meaningful old age than our generation is currently having. After all, we produced the Baby Boomers who are running our country but who, too, are beginning to grow old and sick.

It is time for today's elders to describe publicly their personal experiences as they seek good health care, appropriate housing and social networks. Many caregivers do their best to advocate for us, but we need to speak for ourselves. We, the consumers, must push society to reform the eldercare system.

I am one old woman speaking up.

Working to make the world better for our children – isn't that what loving mothers, fathers, uncles and aunts are supposed to do?

Special thanks to Imogene Higbie for contributing to this chapter with these reflections on her own nursing home experience. The authors thank her for communicating her experience as a way to advocate for millions of others who share her story.

Regulatory Impact on Change

Imogene Higbie speaks for millions of others, many who cannot speak for themselves. But as a society, we stopped listening for so long we've become deaf.

Out of our deafness arose and flourished a rigorous regulatory system so ominous in the nursing home culture it has become like the tail that wags the dog. Although providers are discovering a new path that will antiquate current oversight methods, charting a course through today's regulatory interpretations, surveys and punitive enforcements is risky and difficult. Nonetheless, these challenges do not prevent the transformation we advocate.

In fact, the Omnibus Budget Reconciliation Act of 1987 (OBRA 87) calls for standards consistent with those advocated by the culture change movement regarding resident choice and interdisciplinary approaches to service. Also, certain aspects of culture transformation are officially supported by the Department of Health and Human Services' Center for Medicare/Medicaid Services (CMS). In its most recent 8th Scope of Work, CMS designed an education program to encourage providers to adopt practices to change the culture of their nursing homes. In its promotional video highlighting the Pioneer Network, a national organization that is creating culture change in aging services across the country, CMS highlights the value of such practices and states, "The time has come" for deep-rooted change and surveyors should not stand in its way. For a large bureaucracy, this stance is especially bold and visionary.

The Nursing Home Survey and Enforcement System is Broken

But while the CMS flagship steers in one direction, the rest of the fleet sails in another as if following a different compass. Federal and state survey and enforcement divisions are not yet consistently on the same course to the future, and apparently the incongruity between the direction they are headed and the expressed desire for change is yet to be reconciled. While it is true the nursing home system is broken, the survey and enforcement system is broken alongside it.

In all fairness, there are multiple arms and legs within any large regulatory bureaucracy, and the job of regulating America's nearly 16,500 nursing homes is enormous. In addition, there are bad apples among providers in the industry, so some could argue that we have made our own bed. But it is time for us all to make a new bed.

We know there is a problem with how service is currently provided.

"While the regulatory system is rigorous, it does not prevent the changes we advocate. In fact, OBRA 87 calls for changes consistent with the culture change movement in relation to resident choice."

"While it is true the nursing home system is broken, the survey and enforcement system is broken alongside it."

But instead of fixing it, we continually refine and hone a regulatory process that blindly looks past unnatural, regimented and cold environments and services that drain the life out of people, while using carefully designed systems to root out infractions.

The irony is that nursing homes, while in dire need of change for reasons other than survey outcomes, produce higher clinical standards than do hospitals. If hospitals had the same inspection system as nursing homes and the same public reporting of results, people would be afraid to enter them.

Hospitals have minimal paper-based inspections because the hospital industry has an enormously powerful membership association and political lobby. It is said that nursing homes are the most regulated industry, second only to nuclear power. Inspection consequences are unforgiving. Infractions are publicly reported in extreme language designed to reinforce fear. The culture of inspections, while sometimes civil, is punitive.

The unfortunate truth is that many providers, right or wrong, are afraid to make deep change for fear of negative regulatory consequences.

Paradoxically, it is not unusual for facilities like the one described by Imogene Higbie to be deficiency-free and have solid survey compliance and performance. If they comply with the regulations, their slate is clean. No matter that people are awakened on a time schedule, bathed by hoist and dip, and lined up for rigidly scheduled mealtimes.

On their way to inspect infection rates and safety outcomes, regulators and providers alike will walk past slumping and vacantly detached residents. Both are blind to the reality that no infection is more invasive, no condition more unsafe than the loss of self as perpetuated by the current nursing home culture. Elders' loss of self has been the norm for so long, the regulatory system looks past it in search of non-compliance and infractions. If slumping residents don't fall, have no bed sores, stay hydrated, have no outward symptoms of physical pain and infections are controlled or prevented, their care providers will be viewed by regulators as being in compliance.

"On their way to inspect infection rates and safety outcomes, regulators and providers alike will walk past slumping and vacantly detached residents."

Punitive Systems Do Not Produce Desired Results

While regulations are necessary, punitive oversight systems are not the answer for improving long-term care. Punitive systems have shown no history of creating positive change in any setting, yet we keep sharpening the teeth of the nursing home regulatory system. The federal survey and enforcement system is no longer looking for trends; it now looks for and

"Punitive systems have shown no history of creating positive change in any setting, yet we keep sharpening the teeth of the nursing home regulatory system."

cites situational imperfections. State agencies know it, but they also know that federal surveyors who review state survey results will follow up behind them. Federal oversight and comparative surveys of state agencies grading surveyors on how well they capture *all* deficient practices perpetuate this trend. Although it could be argued that this process serves a purpose, the most common scopes cited are those with "potential for harm."

Above all, regulators do not adequately measure what is most important to people living in nursing homes: Quality of life. *How do I feel about my life? Do I control my own life? Do I eat what and when I want? Do I decide the rules in my own house? Do I have purpose?* Even if regulators ask these questions, rarely is it truly followed up on and/or supported by actual citations in order to draw attention to true quality of life issues.

Instead, regulators measure mechanical care and deem it appropriate if it is provided in a mechanical fashion. Dr. Bill Thomas, a Harvard trained physician and founder of the Eden Alternative, says it best: Medical treatment should be the servant of genuine human caring, never its master. The survey and enforcement system perpetuates clinical treatment as the "master."

Correctly implemented, the Household Model and other deep culture change methods can easily satisfy residents, families, physicians and staff. The Household Model provides what everybody has been starving for all along. Ironically, the struggle now is to satisfy government. Experience shows that providers adopting new approaches consistent with the Household Model will have their day of struggle with the regulatory system. This is an evolutionary reality over which we must not lose heart.

Pioneering Organizations Must Take the Regulatory Risk

Provider organizations that lead in implementing the Household Model and other deep change strategies have discovered many new realities while cutting "wagon-ruts" into virgin prairie. They have learned it truly is possible to replace regimented systems with resident-directed systems; anecdotal evidence abounds about how doing so dramatically improves residents' quality of life.

They also discovered that replacing old militaristic management approaches with coaching, teaching and resource bearing leadership can yield great results. Staff turnover rates usually drop considerably. Resident satisfaction soars. Families become more involved and engaged. Staff becomes passionate about what they do and pour their hearts into truly helping elders reclaim home and the authorship of their own life stories.

However, deep change is a monumental thing in a deeply indoctrinated, regulated and entrenched system like long-term care. Until the whole nursing home sector, including state and national associations and regulatory bodies, redesign support systems to help normalize changes proven successful by innovative providers, individual organizations will continue to require extraordinary energy to transform their cultures. All systems supporting the nursing home – dining, housekeeping, clinical and purchasing services, to name a few – must be retooled to fit a new context. To date, no retooled support systems exist in the long-term care marketplace.

The early pioneers of the Household Model have had to be driven by passion and fortitude, knowing that they are on hallowed but shaky ground. When an organization passionately pushes against a deep norm, the pendulum tends to swing too far in the direction they seek in order to establish new realities. During an advanced phase of organizational evolution, successful Household Model (and other culture change organizations) can become so relaxed in the comfortable, homey environments they have created, they become too lax in meeting basic standards of practice.

For example, employees in small household kitchens that have the aromas, sounds and feel of their own kitchens at home may behave as they do at home rather than routinely and properly washing their hands between functions. The regulatory system has no tolerance for it, nor should it. However, data from pioneering organizations indicate it is a predictable part of the change process that must be lived through and readjusted.

Regulators and Providers Must Find Equilibrium

The problem is, systems in the traditional model were designed for an old context of "We know what's best for you," "This is our place and you fit our rules" and "We provide clinical intervention as we see fit on our schedule not yours."

Many of the old tasks must continue, but they must be altered, adjusted and redesigned within the new context of "What is best for you?" "This is your home, how can we best serve you" and "We provide services to you with your permission at a time that works for you."

Otherwise, transferring the old systems used as they were originally designed into the new Household Model will pull an organization that is trying to change back into its old ways. New systems are called for

"The early pioneers of the Household Model have had to be driven by passion and fortitude, knowing that they are on hallowed but shaky ground."

that anchor the organization in important standards of practice yet fit the philosophies and practices that characterize the new culture. Providing these systems is a primary reason for this book and the accompanying kit components. Most of the critical systems, including infection control, quality assurance, dining and clinical services, MDS procedures and others have been assembled and presented within this kit, redesigned to fit the context of the Household Model. The regulatory system must and surely will, over time, redesign the tools in their chest to better fit this new way. It's the between-now-and-then period that creates risk for change agent organizations.

"There is a natural tension between complying with regulations, standards of practice and 'creating home' with residents…but this tension can and must lead to the creation of very effective care delivery within a humane system," says Patricia Maben, former Director of Long Term Care, Kansas Department on Aging. "Front running pioneers are the ones who must have courage to find and establish that balance. And they need to know that the system may not be friendly to them in the process."

We must recognize we are in the throes of change at all levels of long-term care. Presently, CMS and state survey processes do not place nearly enough value on the truly remarkable and visible quality of life improvements resulting from the Household Model and similar strategies. Nonetheless, CMS has recently published updated interpretive guidelines around quality of life indicators and outcomes for the survey process. There are already many quality of life regulations in place, but states are in the process of implementing these new interpretive guidelines that, in some instances, are consistent with culture change values, principles and methodologies.

Although this signals a shifting of the tide, Household Model provider organizations (together comprising a small minority in the long-term care arena) are still finding their legs amidst deep sea change. Systems like the ones provided in this kit will help, but more are needed.

"Even while outwardly supporting change, the regulatory system has no tolerance for the inevitable evolutionary struggles that must occur as transformational and pioneering organizations break ground for the entire industry."

Even while outwardly supporting change, the regulatory system seems to have little or no tolerance for the inevitable evolutionary struggles that must occur as transformational and pioneering organizations break ground for the entire industry.

Within the decade, the regulatory system most likely will hold all nursing homes accountable for many of the new principles advocated herein, while the number of providers adopting deep change methodologies will increase dramatically. This will bring about more commercially produced, complimentary systems that support these methodologies, and normalization no doubt will occur.

All Must Change; Not Just Providers

For the culture of nursing homes to truly change in a sustainable way, however, all stakeholders must change in similar ways. As CMS and state regulatory agencies begin requiring changes, they are obligated to consider these same changes within their own systems. The regulatory system they ultimately establish, while it should have the teeth to deal strongly with providers who do not routinely comply, should also focus on educating, coaching, and assisting providers during and between surveys as a primary methodology for ensuring quality. Such a system would be effective while creating a partnership in mission and purpose.

Know this: Providers cannot be the only modelers of change and continue having the strain of regulatory consequence on their backs without partnership commitment. Lack of partnership in the change evolution will result in failure or mitigated success.

A father with belt in hand may get his children to mind in the moment, but that is all he will get. He won't have a healthy child no matter how strictly he insists on healthy behavior. A father who wants deep change and growth has to set the example--he has to be what he desires for his children. Realizing the full potential of deep change can and will occur only when all stakeholder groups make the same change.

Undoubtedly, there are risks in creating change consistent with the principles of the Household Model and the culture change movement within our current regulatory environment. Nonetheless, radical changes not only are worth the risk, they are necessary. Providers must take the first step. Risk taking is part of the making of "wagon-ruts" referred to in the Foreword. They are needed to ensure other stakeholders will follow suit.

An undeniable awakening is spreading across the land in long-term care. Regulations will neither produce nor prevent this emerging reality. The spirit of change in the way elders are served has been born and is growing and flourishing.

Objectively identifying and facing up to the status quo is the first step on the pathway to transformation.

Moving toward the solutions is the second step. A clear vision of what *can be* is what truly motivates us to actually change. We must see

"Providers cannot be the only modelers of change and continue having the strain of regulatory consequence on their backs without partnership commitment."

"An undeniable awakening is spreading across our land. Regulations will neither produce nor prevent this emerging reality."

and understand what we can move towards before we can let go of what we have. Regulations or no regulations, we must replace institution with home.

chapter 3
Home Is a
Basic Necessity

"As far as we can discern, the sole purpose of human existence is to kindle
a light of meaning in the darkness of mere being."
- Carl Gustav Jung

We need to remember what home means in our own lives. For most of us, home is a basic necessity for a wholesome and balanced life. It is where we retreat, regroup and find sustenance.

Home is, in fact, an extension of our self-identity, which we alone create. Whether our persona is that of a painfully shy person or life-of-the-party, it is the one with which we establish our place in the world. Nowhere is our self-identity reinforced more than at home.

For this reason, the Household Model sets great store in the belief that the creation of a true home for elders is paramount. There are some who may question that it is a fundamental building block for long-term care. Here we attempt to firmly establish the importance of home as an essential need for all, at all times.

During our lifetimes we may have lived in several different houses, but each was our home because we made it so with our rituals, routines and personal touch. No matter where we lived, we took control by working to create a comfortable living space suited to our particular needs and tastes - one that reflects who we are.

We continue to assume control over our home environment after we retire. These are our golden years, our reward for a life of hard work. We spend years talking about what we are going to do when we retire. Our plans are endless and all appeal to our unique sense of self. Though the plans are filled with adventure, there is an unspoken assumption of home. Home is the place we will come back to, where we will rest between expeditions, where we will detail the plans of the next phase. Home is not necessarily the house we lived in while working – but wherever it is, however it is configured, it will be home. It will be a reflection of self. Within it will be all that we need. Finally, we will be able to enjoy our home to the fullest.

This post retirement period is also the time when we most need the stability of home and the sense of self it provides, for this typically is not only a time for new discoveries, but a time of profound loss. Retirement can diminish our feeling of self worth because we consider ourselves less useful than when we were employed. Social support slips as friends and family members die or move away. Our health may decline and perhaps we become more dependent on others.

We feel guilty when we have to ask our loving but busy daughter for a ride to church. We feel old and in the way when our grandchildren frown impatiently as they help us into the car.

Still, as long as we live at home – even if it is a small apartment or a condo – we retain control over our life and respect from friends and relatives. Our children tell their friends, "Mom and Dad decided to move out of that big old house and are living in senior housing. Actually, it's quite nice. Now they can travel and never worry about their yard."

But the mood changes when we are admitted to a nursing home: "We had to place mom in a nursing home. It's been really hard. You know how persnickety she was about her house - everything had to be just the way she liked. She always loved to cook and now she can't even go into the kitchen. I told her 'Mom, you just have to sit back and let others do for you.' "

Relationships with family members change. They feel uncomfortable visiting us in this strange new environment with the lack of privacy it affords. Conversations are strained as we struggle to find something in common to discuss. The things we used to talk about – the yard, the birds, the dog, the leaky faucet, the neighbors, plans for a small party, friends at church – are gone or so far away they seem unimportant.

Compounding the trauma of moving into an alien environment is a sense of denial. When elders come into nursing homes, they often arrive in a waiting mode much like when they enter a hospital. They tell themselves, "I'm just here for a while *then* I'm going home." They do not acknowledge it, but many will wait the rest of their lives.

Their expectation of eventually returning home obscures the reality of their situation, so they forfeit even the choice to surrender to their new surroundings. While they wait, the all-pervasive institution with its assembly-line culture diminishes their individuality and their power of self. If we feel a bit cowed visiting the doctor's office, think how intimidated elders must feel residing permanently amid the hustle and bustle of a nursing home.

When we are admitted to a nursing home, we are no longer expected – or allowed – to be in control.

"Mom, you just have to sit back and let others do for you."
Translation: *"You are done. Stop being yourself."*

Home is Self

A group of researchers and practitioners struggled together recently to identify the domains of well-being embedded so naturally in our lifestyles of home. In their work, *Well-being Beyond Quality of Life, a Metamorphosis of Eldercare,* the authors spoke of seven domains of well-being: identity,

"Mom, you just have to sit back and let others do for you."
Translation: "You are done. Stop being yourself."

growth, autonomy, security, connectedness, meaning and joy.   All appear to change as the frail elder enters into the institutional system of care. The authors state that the risks of slipping from a state of well-being "increases dramatically for nursing home residents disconnected from the past by loss of familiar places and personal possessions, and from the future by loss of hopes and dreams."

When talking about ourselves we speak the language of these domains of well-being, but we rarely consider that these are also the gifts of home. The house we love to drive up to, the yard of sunshine and rain, the porch that boundaries the stranger, the kitchen and coffee pot that welcomes the neighbor, the chair and cushion under the reading lamp, the bath that soothes and pleasures, the freedom of movement from room to room, the old box of photos and the treasures always available in the attic to remind us of the life we've led - all are merely the accoutrements of home. But when they are gone, the deeper sense of well-being embedded in home is endangered as well.

Losing Home, Losing Self

Living in an institutional care environment we resign ourselves to this loss. The losses are often compounded as time goes on. Even the ability to walk is frequently sacrificed to the needs of the system. There is a schedule to keep and no time to shuffle with a walker to the dining room, so elders are put into a wheelchair and whisked down the corridor until they lose all ability to walk.

We once heard a nurse aide call out to a resident who was trying to stand up, "Sit down. Your walking days are over." The aide was in fact a very loving woman, and we feel sure she had no idea of the harshness of her words.

Having no obvious purpose but to be cared for – i.e., warehoused until shipped out – the elder's self-identity seeps away, unnoticed at first, until none of the original identity is left around which to organize. The elder's diagnosis and room number becomes his or her identity.

We suspect if a time-lapse video were made following an elder's entry into a traditional nursing home it would show much the same progression (or rather, regression) as a wilting flower. The final frames would reveal what is commonly known in long-term care as "slumping." The elder with vacant eyes drools and slouches in a wheelchair as if the body, like an old car, has been abandoned by the driver.

"The elder's diagnosis and room number becomes his or her identity."

When residents arrive at that state, we attend to them, but unconsciously disregard them as persons, focusing our emotional energies instead on those who have not yet lost themselves. It is from the latter we take the strength needed to sustain our work in a system that is just as repressive to us as it is to them. Unlike the residents who have succumbed, we survive because we have a measure of control and more stamina, which unfortunately we use to perpetuate the system.

Many would argue that slumping is the result of age and disease. Yet, we have witnessed time after time how the condition reverses and elders begin to blossom once the warehousing approach to nursing care is replaced by environments elders can identify as "home."

We can't feel a sense of wholeness, safety and belonging, exercise autonomy, experience joy, build community or fully actualize without the sanctuary of home.

Homelessness: A Reality of Nursing Homes

To support this premise of loss of home, we rarely hear residents describe the facility they live in as "home." Rather, they wistfully speak of home as something in the past stripped forever from their grasp. They talk longingly and unrealistically about "going home." When relatives come to visit, they may find their loved one in the doorway with purse in hand, pleading to go home.

The reason is simple; no one views a nursing home as a true home for those living there. For us who work there, it is *our* place, not theirs. *We* run it. *We* make the decisions. Further logical analysis leads to only one conclusion; people who reside in nursing homes are homeless with a roof over their heads.

Research at a nursing home in Connecticut by Judith Carboni, RN, MSN, CS, reinforces the idea that institutionalized elders are in effect homeless. She defines home as "a fluid and dynamic intimate relationship between the individual and the environment...a lived experience that possesses deep existential meaning for the individual."

What she found was just the opposite:

"When one is homeless, there is no private place to which one can withdraw, and this lack of privacy was evident for all residents of the nursing home. There seemed to be no retreat to call one's own, save for a retreat into self.

Homelessness engenders feelings of powerlessness and dependency. These feelings were predominantly experienced by the (resident) informants. They were aware that the institution, not they, made the rules, and that routine dominated the day. As a result of this lack of autonomy and imposition of rules, informants demonstrated increasing inability to make decisions for themselves.

Endless repetition directed their lives and meaningless tasks seemed to add to the numbness that resulted in boredom and low energy. Both informants and group members shared feelings of anxiety, fearfulness, and uncertainty, indicating that to be in an institution and homeless is to be insecure in an uncertain world; it is to be filled with doubts and to be a stranger.

To not have a home is to not have a safe haven in which to find protection. When one is homeless, one is vulnerable and in danger at all times. This clearly describes both informants and the majority of nursing home residents who say little, disclose even less, and distrust most people around them."

Observe the striking similarities in the posture and demeanor of a homeless person on the street to that of a slumping elder parked at the nurses' station. Neither have control over their physical space or a way to shut out the world other than to mentally disengage and escape deep within. It is as if slumping, with eyes downcast and vacant, is their way of locking the door.

Passersby treat slumping elders and bag ladies much the same. When we cross paths with one of the latter, do we make eye contact, smile and say "what a lovely day" as we would to a well-dressed stranger we encounter on the street? What keeps us from doing so? Perhaps because we have already made up our minds about the person based on her outward appearance, or maybe we are afraid she is going to ask something of us. The unconventional dress and demeanor of the homeless make us ill at ease, and we begin to see them more as objects than as persons.

We objectify elders who slump in much the same way. They make us feel uncomfortable, or maybe we just don't have time to stop and acknowledge them as we delve into our paperwork or hurry to the next meeting. But what must it feel like from their point of view? Do they think we don't see them or don't care; that they're living alone in a crowd?

It becomes a downward spiral: the elders feel even more disengaged and invisible, leading to further discomfort and aloofness on the part of staff.

"If the consequence of being institutionalized is to be homeless, and if to be homeless is to lack meaning in life and to suffer intolerable pain, then can we justify providing and promoting this negative experience for the vulnerable and chronically ill elderly individual?"
--Judith Carboni

Failing health should not render us homeless. Depriving a person of a need so fundamental as home, even with the best of intentions, violates a basic human right.

Begin at Home to Create Home

We must begin at home to create a home. When we, as long-term care leaders begin changing the culture of nursing homes in our own communities, everybody and everything else will follow suit.

The industrial assembly line of care must be eradicated in this home we work to create. Life-long possessions, simple pleasures and routines must be re-instated to each unique person living in a nursing home. The hallway outside the bedrooms must no longer be a public street where complete strangers can walk by and where others, known only by name badges, can walk into residents' rooms at any moment without knocking. Dignity must be returned to the bathing experience, eliminating the embarrassing trip down the busy corridor in a wheelchair wearing only a nightgown and the "hoist and dip" bathing method that treats humans like boxes of widgets.

We must design home that acts in tandem with the lifestyle and tastes of those living within. The physical layout must stimulate the cultural norms of privacy, relationships, autonomy and pleasure so that each person who lives within will have the opportunity to be at home.

Moving Toward a Future of Possibilities

Now that we have faced the reality of today in these early chapters, the balance of this book begins a pathway for you to take the nursing home system you have inherited and reshape it into something whole and healthy, thereby creating a deep, lasting legacy in your community. The information in the following pages will enable you to transform lives, including your own, in ways that will humble and astound you, and liberate legions of elders and caregivers you will never meet.

Does life have a stronger measure?

"Failing health should not render us homeless. Depriving a person of a need so fundamental as home, even with the best of intentions, violates a basic human right. "

chapter 4
The Essential Elements of the Household Model

"Home is not where you live, but where they understand you."
- Christian Morganstern

The fragrance of warm muffins and hot coffee drew me to the door of Ptacek House, one of six newly established healthcare households within the community of Meadowlark Hills. I rang the doorbell and Susan, a household employee, answered the door and welcomed me in. I saw a warmly furnished living room and an adjacent kitchen and dining room; all appointed like any other home in America. The residents, an average of sixteen per household, had moved in less than two weeks before.

The signs of home were already visible amid what previously had been public corridors, cramped bedrooms and large public gathering rooms. The institutional odor was gone. My stomach growled in response to the smells of breakfast floating from the household kitchen that made me want to see "what's cooking." The previous set of monotonous, unit style chairs, tables and other office-like trappings had gone to the auction block to make way for more cozy furnishings. Each household had re-arranged its initial set of new furniture to reflect the emerging lifestyle patterns of the people who lived there.

People were visiting with one another and, in stark contrast to the dismal scene of slumping, slumbering elders once parked at the now-dismantled nurses' station, a more inspiring dance of life unfolded. My heart warmed with hope. The transformation was like a new marriage for all of us...the intense excitement, depth of emotion and commitment of love coupled with fears of inadequacy and the uncertainty of the "yet to be."

But all the blossoming signs of home faded into the background when my eyes found Lee Chung Hi, the lady who screams. She had abandoned her Geri-chair and was sitting comfortably at the dining table, just as my wife had sat at our kitchen table when I left home for work that morning.

It was the first time I had seen Lee Chung Hi when she wasn't screaming.

She was smiling. Her eyes locked with mine, conveying a warmth of wellbeing that sent me into a suspended sense of time and place. All I could see was her warm smile and radiating eyes of peace, and I felt myself walking toward her as if in slow motion.

I stopped near her table. With her hands at her side, she bowed her head slowly forward and then back up, all the while continuing her smile. This gesture of greeting and respect, practiced in her culture yet universally understood, enveloped my whole being. I found myself returning the gesture in full communion. I was able to return eye contact and nod in mutual affirmation before emotion overtook me.

The sum of our enormous effort to overcome a broken system – the months and months of striving in a community-wide commitment born of a belief there *must* be something better – was distilled through Lee Chung Hi's graceful and simple bow. It shook me to the core.

Her years of screaming, contrasted with the moment we had just shared, represented to me everything we must leave behind and everything we must achieve. The glaring reality was she hadn't screamed for years because she was sick, but because *we* were.

In screaming, Lee Chung Hi had used her only tool for hanging on to herself rather than giving in to vacant slumping. She was a fighter—a screaming indictment of the traditional nursing home system and proof in the pudding that we *can* overcome; that we have a moral imperative to do so.

Like so many other milestones along Meadowlark Hills' difficult road to the Household Model, Lee Chung Hi's bow was a validation and gift of encouragement. It was as if she had said, "This is right. Keep going!"

Clouds of doubt hovered over each of us at some point along our journey. But that moment with Lee Chung Hi brought me personal resolve and commitment to keep moving forward. I will never forget it.

Home: A Sanctuary Where Grace Abounds

If life was just about the passing of time, we might not mind so much standing in line or sitting in waiting rooms, traffic jams, airports and the DMV. Do you know anyone who looks forward to these minutes (that seem like hours) surrounded by strangers and subject to someone else's timetable? Probably not. Instead, we seek to fill our lives with enriching, sensual and joyful experiences - habitual or new, planned or spontaneous. It's no different for frail elders.

Creating home as our sanctuary and the place that fosters graceful living happens naturally and subtly over time. We may not think of the work or decisions that occur everyday to sustain our home, but there is no doubt it is *we* who direct its development. Being in charge of our own home brings meaning and priceless quality to our life and enables our individual potential to flourish.

Because home is such a *basic* necessity, we take it for granted. Consequently we don't adequately consider all the essential elements of the homes we help create for frail elders. There is no sanctuary or graceful living in the traditional nursing home model created by "us" for "them."

"Creating home as our sanctuary and the place that fosters graceful living happens naturally and subtly over time."

The elders in households must be in the driver's seat as they create their own home. We have a responsibility to be their partners in this pursuit.

The regimens of the traditional nursing home model tightly control the possibilities in daily life. The biggest difference between home and institutional living is that home allows endless ways for a day to play out - a myriad of little things to add spice to life. Some we choose, others fall at our feet. There is a unique anticipation of "what's next." The organic rituals of our days grow from the many variables that cross our paths, whether in joy or sorrow. The Household Model welcomes these variables. Our seeking opens the window to the gift of grace.

Values and Beliefs Shape Essential Elements of the Household Model

The Household Model requires self-change, transformative leadership, redesign of the organization and reconstruction of the physical environment to produce true home. Values and beliefs are the threads that weave these together to create the fabric of life within the home.

Just as we choose values and beliefs to guide our own lives, so, too, must we choose them to lead our organizations. We err deeply by organizing ourselves around business principles. We think (and many business schools teach) that enterprises are primarily driven by numbers, policies and efficient practices. These are important for any business, but they cannot be the drivers. Rather, purpose, values, principles and beliefs must drive the organization. They must collectively lay the foundation for any enterprise that desires to stand tall in its field.

For example, putting customers in the driver's seat and ensuring satisfaction in their experience is a fundamental value. Operating systems, while important, are merely tools for carrying out the purpose for the company's existence. They cannot stand on their own unless driven by beliefs.

Absence of stated beliefs and values are by default statements of beliefs and values. Many companies operate without them. Erroneously, they are associated with not-for-profit entities. A growing number of very successful for-profit companies that are viewed warmly by the marketplace are driven by clearly stated and consistently lived values and beliefs.

The culture of business teaches us, perhaps unintentionally, that the "soft" words characteristic of values are suspect. They make us uncomfortable in business settings. We like hard words like "budget," "policy," "forecast" and "schedule." Those words make us feel efficient,

"The elders in households must be in the driver's seat as they create their own home. We have a responsibility to be their partners in this pursuit."

responsible and effective. We may *feel* that way, but it is not necessarily true.

Values and beliefs are the soul of the organization. An organization that serves people in residence 24 hours a day must especially be filled with soul in all that it is and does.

Consequently, it should be no surprise that the Household Model is driven by values and beliefs. They are the essential elements in the household's design and purpose. The entire organization, its people and physical design must be driven by these "Essential Elements." They are the marrow within the bones of it all. While they are not religious statements, they must be religiously lived. The words may sound soft, but when lived out they give the strength of steel to the Household Model.

Household Model Framework

The framework of the **traditional nursing home model** could be described as follows:

Staff, systems, policy and regulation driven service to frail elders in residence, who must subjugate themselves to fit within the framework of highly regimented and scheduled services that are delivered through departmental silos of top-down management within a public institutional setting.

The framework of the **Household Model** could be described as:

Small groups of people sharing house and home while directing their own daily lives through a responsive, highly valued and decentralized self-led service team that is supported by values-driven, resource-bearing leadership philosophies, practices, policies and systems.

The Essential Elements

The Essential Elements are the foundation of the Household Model. They are the guide and inspiration of the journey. The goal is for elders to one day take these principles for granted just as we take for granted the comfort of walking through our own front door.

> "Values and beliefs are the soul of the organization."

> "The goal is for elders to one day take these principles for granted just as we take for granted the comfort of walking through our own front door."

ESSENTIAL ELEMENTS

1. The household is each resident's home and sanctuary.

2. The people who live here direct their own lives, individually and collectively.

3. The boundaries of the person and his/her home are clear and respected as a matter of course.

4. Grace, a shared sense of what is sacred about the house and its people, is deeply valued, consciously created and preserved. Ritual, spontaneity, friendship, spirituality, celebration, recreation, choice, interdependence, art and humor are all manifestations of a culture of grace.

5. The people who live here are loved and served by a responsive, highly valued, decentralized, self-led service team that has responsibility and authority.

6. Leadership is a characteristic, not a position. Leaders support and are supported by values-driven, resource bearing principles and practices as a way for each person to actualize his or her full potential.

7. All systems, including treatments, exist to support and serve the person, within the context of his or her life pursuits.

8. We build strong community with one another, our family, our neighbors and our town. Each household is part of a neighborhood of houses, dedicated to continuous learning.

9. The physical building and all its amenities are designed to be a true home. Institutional creep in design and culture is treated as a wolf at the door.

The Essential Elements must be our aspiration. Living up to them requires deep and profound change by all of us in how we think, plan and act in regard to every aspect of long-term care. The first step of the journey begins within your own heart and with your personal understanding of change.

chapter 5
Change - It's Everywhere

"Be not afraid of growing slowly. Be only afraid of standing still."
- Chinese Proverb

Life itself is change. We change, as does everything around us. Change is constant, pervasive and irreversible. Some change is measurable, such as growth and decay. Other change is more abstract: the way we become a bit more knowledgeable and experienced everyday, the way our preferences adjust or the way a relationship becomes more open or distant. We barely think about gradual, everyday, common changes like these from one minute to the next. Only months later do we notice the children have grown or that we have become adept at a skill. We accept these changes as part of life and would be surprised if they didn't happen. No big decision or catalyst is made. It is just the evolution of matter and mind through time.

Though we almost always try to resist change, doing so is futile. Time marches on, dragging transformation in its wake. Every moment – different from the last – creates its own unique opportunity for change, and then is forever gone. It takes a certain set of circumstances to even begin to envision change. Then, things begin to fall into place and a window of opportunity opens for creating change. This takes time. Having a little wind at your back doesn't hurt, either.

It may seem elemental to illustrate that change is inevitable and that we often try in vain to resist it. Nonetheless, here we will discuss it in depth so that we can begin to create a relationship with the idea of change before actually beginning to experience it. Because, as we have found on our own change journeys, the only way to embrace change and not be victimized by it is to be involved in it.

Change Is Everybody's Job

Creating a lasting change in an organization requires profound transformation of the ruling structure. The human force shaping the future must not manage from above, but lead from within. Leadership must view change as a vital life force and embrace it. The role of leadership is to work enthusiastically to accomplish change. Anyone, and preferably everyone involved can take on leadership roles.

Jan Carlzon, former president of Scandinavian Airlines systems said, "An individual without information cannot take responsibility; with information can not help but take responsibility." Change is eveybody's job – throughout the organization.

"The only way to embrace change and not be victimized by it is to be involved in it."

All or Nothing

Because of the human dynamic involved, the change needed to sustain progress in long-term care needs to be deep. That is, it needs to be changed (transformed) to be changing (a state of being; not just one thing, but many things).

As Tom Peters offers in his book, *Design*, "Incrementalism is *Out*. Destruction is *In*. 'Continuous improvement,' the lead mantra of the 1980s management, is now downright dangerous. All or nothing. ('Control. Alt. Delete.') We must gut the innards of our enterprises before new competitors do it for us – and to us."

Our journey to change long-term care must be far reaching, transforming the quality of interactions on the individual level between staff and elders, among service areas and functions, within the organization as a whole and throughout the industry itself. The change must be profound so there is no mistaking intentions. There is a reason the movement is called "culture change" and not "culture adjustment" or "old culture, new suit" or "same culture, different paperwork." Changes need to be from small and specific to grand and broad sweeping and they must all somehow interplay and complement each other.

Change *imposed* on elders and staff will likely be superficial, un-welcomed and inappropriate. It will not be truly assimilated into the culture but mindlessly adhered to like so many other routines and protocols. Conversely, when elders and staff work together as leaders to strategize and implement change, they take ownership of the transformation. It becomes easier to predict and prepare for the twists and turns in the road ahead. When something goes awry, they may see it as a crisis, but they persevere because they have control in finding solutions. Rather than feeling isolated and powerless, they gain through collaboration a sense of creativity, adventure and inspiration that enables them to embrace change and the challenges it brings.

The change is not simply from a model resembling an institution to one resembling a home. Rather, it is deep change from living institutionally – where one size fits all and individuality is sacrificed by obeisance to regulations and operational regimentation – to living in a way that honors each individual's idea of home. The concept of home varies from person to person and over time may even change for the individual. Thus, there is no cookie-cutter approach to creating home with and for elders. While the Household Model claims fundamental principles and framework which must be adhered to, it is not prescriptive and does not require each organization to design and implement it exactly the same way. It is not like a McDonald's franchise where a Quarter Pounder™ tastes the same in Los Angeles as it does in Washington D.C. Each facility must find its own recipe, devised by the people who live there. The local culture and flavor must find its own expression in each new emerging household in each town. Architecture will vary, staff configurations will vary, and numbers of residents in each house will vary depending upon local variables. On an individual level, staff in all households and various service areas must be responsible for finding how best to foster the freedom of home with each resident.

Breakpoint Change

Every so often a change so big occurs it turns everything on its head. In the book, *Breakpoint and Beyond,* George Lamb and Beth Jarman call this "breakpoint change." It is a change so different from anything preceding it that it demolishes normal standards. Breakpoint change is not incremental change or continuous improvement. At breakpoint, change is so sharp the old rules no longer apply and continuing to use them will result in failure.

Take the rise of cell phones and the Internet for example. These days it is rare for a company not to have a webpage or email. Cell phones are so prevalent, some individuals and companies no longer use a landline. Originally, these technologies gave companies an edge. Now, it is so common that in most cases operating without them puts the company at a serious disadvantage. Not only did the technology change the workplace environment, it also changed our vision of the world and the rules of the game.

Breakpoint Change: The Household Model

The philosopher Jose Ortega y Gasset said, "Life is a series of collisions with the future; it is not a sum of what we have been, but what we yearn to be." Is the current state of long-term care what we yearn it to be? Hopefully not. Lucky for us, it is not the past that will define us, but the future we envision. The future of long-term care is elder directed homes, not business institutions. When we hit the breakpoint, there will be no turning back. Choice will be as commonplace as email. Home environments will be the norm. We will look back at a time when we warehoused our elders with much the same disbelief in which we now behold the age of slavery. It will be unacceptable.

The Household Model is breakpoint change. While struggles abound in the industry as we untangle from the shackles of long-established norms, there is no denying that the sands are shifting in ways not felt before.

We are running out of time for feeling this luxury of evaluating the merits of deep culture change, and if we do not proactively embrace new ways our organizations will not survive the next decade. Unlike virtually everything around us, long-term care has somehow sheltered itself in a cocoon of status quo for decades. But the waters of change have been simmering for some time. We are reaching a boiling point. When that point is reached, the entire face of the industry will change rapidly leaving those hesitant to change and reposition out in the cold.

Once that grand change is made, old ways and old systems will no longer fit and it will be impossible to go back to them. The system produced by this new order of things will not allow it.

chapter 6
A Map for Change

"Life wants to happen. Life is unstoppable. Anytime we try and contain life, or interfere with its fundamental need for expression, we get into trouble. Many of the dilemmas of our time arise from our inability to honor life's ceaseless urge to be..."
- Margaret J. Wheatley and Myron Kellner-Rogers

We've talked about how change is a journey, not just a flipping of a switch. We would not just drop you off at the crossroads and say, "Good luck!" The next section lays out the processes and stages of change so you will learn where you are in your journey and how to navigate through each stage.

Prochaska's Change Theory

In his book, "Changing for Good," James O. Prochaska, Ph.D. outlines the stages self-changers go through to best transition through a change. He began by looking at therapies to see which was most effective in helping people change problem behavior like smoking, overeating and drinking. He found that all therapies work equally well and that the differences between those who successfully changed and those who did not had to do with the individuals' ability to manage their own change process.

The "Problem Behavior" is Long-term Care Indoctrination

We are drawn to Prochaska's model not only because it is anchored in tested theory about the stages of change, but because it is based on breaking out of addictive behaviors. While long-term care workers may not be in the same dire straits as drug addicts, the attachment to our behaviors and established systems can be as strong. We can't help ourselves. The-way-things-are-done is a habit. Our deep indoctrination to the systems of nursing homes is not so different from addiction. While, like an addict, we may first want to deny it, the difficulty and resistance experienced by organizations and the individuals within them as they contemplate and make change is much like an addict overcoming unhealthy habits and behaviors. The indoctrination of the system and our part in it often becomes wrapped up in our professional identity and holds us back from being all we can be. Change will not come overnight or without intervention; another similarity to addiction.

Prochaska notes that change happens in clearly observable stages over time. The stages are: pre-contemplation, contemplation, preparation, action and maintenance (which we will call "sustainability"). In each stage he found there are tasks that must be completed before moving on to the next stage. We can get stuck in any stage, but once control over it is achieved, we can progress to the next stage. He describes the stages of change and the processes used to move through them.

"Our deep indoctrination to the systems of nursing homes is not so different from addiction."

Change Processes

Processes are different from techniques. In fact, techniques make up processes and are highly individualistic. The main processes for change offered by Prochaska are:

- Consciousness-raising
- Social liberation
- Emotional arousal
- Self-reevaluation
- Commitment
- Countering
- Environmental control
- Rewards
- Helping Relationships

Consciousness-raising: Here you raise your awareness about yourself and the change you are about to undertake. The smoker might read up on the dangers of smoking, collect literature on different quitting techniques and talk to her doctor about her particular risks.

You read up on the Household Model and deep culture change or maybe see a presentation. You start to get in touch with your feelings about how things are run in your facility, what you would like to change about it and what you might change about yourself. You see where you have internal resistance and where you have motivation within yourself.

Social liberation: Social liberation deals with finding outlets in your external environment to help you change. If you were trying to quit smoking, you might sit in non-smoking sections at restaurants or spend time where smoking is not allowed.

If you wish to change long-term care, you might visit a culture change facility for inspiration to see that yes, it can be done. It might mean getting rid of the nursing station to break the habit of it being the center of attention for staff and residents as an indicator of deeper change to come.

Emotional arousal: This process is about getting your emotional self behind the change and finding inspiration in it. An example is when someone is moved to quit smoking after a loved one has died of lung cancer. In a culture change situation you may take time to really *see* residents and think, "This could be *my* mom or *my* grandfather. Or, what if this was *me?*"

Self-reevaluation: Here you think about how your values align with the current system and how these values might realign when you change. You may think of yourself as a caring person but know, given current circumstances, you are not often able to give each resident the personal attention he or she deserves. You examine how you may be resisting change and why. You envision the person you hope to become and think about how that may make you feel, what you will gain and what you must give up.

Commitment: Making a commitment is taking personal responsibility for your own change. You realize the role you and your actions must play for change to happen. The process will not move forward without you. You make the commitment to yourself and then publicly, perhaps by sharing your commitment with others in a learning circle. This shows you and others you work with that you are serious. You know the change will be deep and you are committed to seeing it through. Remembering your commitment will motivate you when the going gets tough, and remind you to not let yourself or others down.

Countering: Countering replaces an unhealthy behavior with a healthy one. For example, if you are trying to lose weight, you may take a walk around the block when you want to go to the fridge for cake. If you find yourself falling into habits of the old model of care, you may take a few minutes to stop and visit with an elder to get you back on track. Or, you might connect with others in the organization for some support and encouragement.

Environmental control: While countering is about dealing with internal obstacles to change, environmental control is about getting a handle on obstacles around you. If you are trying to lose weight you may get rid of all the junk food in the house or steer clear of fast food restaurants or ice cream shops. In your facility, you would get rid of the nurses' station, food trays and other institutional symbols. You might stick a note in your pocket that reads something like "How is this home?" and pull it out when you need a reminder to keep you on the right track.

Rewards: Prochaska says that punishment is not beneficial to change in the long run, but rewards are. Rewards make you feel good about change and remind you change is a positive process. If you are trying to quit smoking, you may put the money you save not buying cigarettes into your own "fun fund." When it gets big enough and you need an extra boost, buy yourself a present. In an organization going through culture change, there are deep personal rewards in a framework that encourages staff visits with residents, perhaps perusing photo albums together, cooking together, watching soap operas, sharing intimate moments of family and dreams, going for walks, "getting out of the house" for the afternoon with a resident or taking a group outing to a local brewery or mall.

Helping relationships: Just because you are working on changing *yourself* does not mean you are out there on your own. Many alcoholics enlist Alcoholics Anonymous to help them on their journey to sobriety.

Your day will not be "business as usual" while undergoing change. Enlist friends and family to lend an ear of encouragement when you are struggling. They can help just by being aware of the stress you are facing and treating you with understanding when you are edgy or tired after a day at work.

Of course, the team is the biggest resource for helping you through change. Scheduling regular learning circles to talk about personal struggles and offer mutual support will help as will avoiding harmful relationships. You may want to steer clear of the pessimistic co-worker who always complains, "This culture change stuff doesn't work" so he doesn't drag you down with him.

Some of these processes are used near the beginning of change, while others come into play once you are well on your way. Some will be used throughout. When you are stuck, refer to this list of processes to find one that may help.

Stages of Change

Prochaska's stages of change outline the change journey. Each stage is significant and has its own lessons to teach. But just because you have a map does not mean you won't encounter obstacles or detours. There can and will be setbacks. However, all hope is not lost. Get back on track by looking at the map and taking inventory of your skills and what you have accomplished so far. Your change journey may seem to progress more quickly by skipping certain stages, but ultimately you will likely need to revisit what you missed. Prochaska found that doing the right things in the right order is key to creating successful, long lasting change.

Pre-contemplation: During this stage, the pre-contemplator cannot see the problem. It is not that the problem is not there, only that he can't or won't acknowledge it. The alcoholic says, "I can quit if I want to. I just don't want to." The smoker says, "I'll quit someday but my life is just too stressful now."

The pre-contemplator in long-term care has heard about deep culture change and the Household Model but says, "Our residents are too sick," or, "You could never do that unless you had a lot more staff," or, "Our residents are happy the way it is," or, "Our residents like a structured and scheduled life."

Perhaps the pre-contemplator ignores the topic all together. (Both authors have experienced situations where the fact was raised that elders, like all of us, need a true home, only to have the words completely and almost comically ignored. Heads turned from the speaker and the topic was completely changed to more comfortable issues like measuring outcomes, clinical protocols or reducing incidents of falls.)

Or, the pre-contemplator may initially like the philosophy of creating home for residents. It sounds great until she realizes creating home means things, including her work, will change forever in profound ways. She thinks, "What about my job? What about me? What happens to the MDS (Minimum Data Set) coordinator if you move the MDS function to the household?" Her mindset slides back into resisting change.

Contemplation: During this stage the contemplator acknowledges he has a problem, struggles to understand it and searches for a solution. Premature, impulsive and half-hearted attempts to change are made. The smoker quits six times in three months. In fact, says Prochaska, many smokers spend up to two years thinking about it before finally quitting. The contemplator recognizes he must change and is both anxious and excited about it.

In long-term care, the contemplator is repulsed by what he sees as he walks down the hall of the nursing home where he works - elders sitting slumped, people calling out. So many so alone. Perhaps he saw a culture change presentation. Since then, he sees things differently. He visits a facility that has created the Household Model. The elders there seem so much more involved and happier than those at his facility. He thinks about his *own* home and why it is so important to him. He can hardly talk of anything else. His wife laughingly says he hangs out more with her in the kitchen and insists the kids sit down for meals and have real conversations.

Resolution of this stage is noticeable when you find yourself focusing more on the solution than on the problem. You begin to think about the future and see how things could be different. You move from passive thinking to active feeling.

Preparation: This stage is filled with serious activity. The changer reduces her nicotine intake by smoking only in the back yard. She reads self-help manuals.

The long-term care nurses' aide decides she can no longer care for elders in the institutional way. It doesn't matter that she works in a traditional nursing home. She becomes personally committed to relating to each and every resident in a new, life-affirming way.

The caregiver says to the supervisor, "Have you heard about this culture change thing? I feel totally different now. I can't look at the residents in the same way ever again. We have to figure out how to create home here!" or "I can no long subscribe to the way we are doing things." By now, the changer is really building up internal momentum. Feelings have graduated to resolve. Resolve has led to planning, sharing, and influencing.

Action: And then, one day, the changer takes the big leap. She behaves differently and it is obvious to others. "Don't you want dessert?" a friend asks quizzically.

The Director of Nursing gathers the staff and says, "Contrary to what I told you before when I said, 'Get back to work,' I do want you to stop and talk to the residents and build meaningful relationships and I'm going to do it too." Staff begins *living* culture change.

Sustainability: Change never ends with the initial action. There is always a risk of slipping backward. If you slip and fall off a horse, the ride is not over. You get back on. It is relatively easy to lose weight. But keeping it off is the real struggle. The alcoholic says it for all self-changers, "One day at a time."

An administrator in a long-term care facility may give a team of caregivers authority to plan a schedule for the household's second shift. But after seeing the schedule they create, she tells them, "No. You can't. It won't work." She slips out of fear of failure and loss of control. The administrator and the team may need to examine that fear and their commitment to change.

Some types of change remain forever at risk of sliding back into the old way of doing things. The maintenance never ends. Our colleague, Linda Bump, arguably the mother of the Household Model, is a continuous inspiration to the authors. She uses four benchmark questions to keep an organization's culture change journey on course. We call it "Bump's Law." We must always ask ourselves, when tempted by assembly-line efficiencies, the questions of Bump's Law:

Bump's Law:

What does the resident want?

How did the resident do it at his/her previous home?

How do *you* do it at home?

How should we do it here?

The Norton-Shields Change Matrix For Progression to Households

The Study of the Matrix

Making the deep and lasting change called for in the Household Model is difficult and complex. Undoing and unlearning is concurrent with redoing, relearning and making new discoveries. Following Prochaska's lead, the authors developed the Norton-Shields Matrix to help guide the change agent through the varied stages and processes required to make the dramatic and profound changes needed in birthing the Household Model within his or her organization.

Linear progression in any profound change is rare. Our Matrix of change allows for a progression that one can understand in multiple ways. If you look at the columns from left to right you will see the stages of change from different vantage points of the organization (personal, leadership, organization, environment). Looking down each column will give you an idea of what the stages of change look like from the different vantage points. These stages are based on J.O Prochaska's *Stages of Change*.

The Matrix can also be used to see an over-all chronology, beginning with an individual who is aware only of the traditional model of nursing home care, and moving to full participation of the facility's residents and staff within the Household Model. Start at the top left, work your way down the column, move to the top of the next column, work your way down, etc. Imagine the path of a sine wave. You will see the progression from the first inkling things must change, to becoming a leader, to inspiring others to lead, to full collaboration in redesigning the organization. Finally, the self-led team of staff works with residents to design and create the living environment, and all are acknowledged and rewarded with continuous opportunity to learn and grow.

The total transformation begins with individual transformation. It is important to ground yourself in the need for personal change as you enter into the world introduced in the Matrix. Most start someplace else, which usually ends in frustration, failure, or mitigated success. We must start with ourselves, look and act within. Only then can we effectively look and act outwardly along the pathway of change. The individual becomes a leader and instigates opportunities for others to experience the personal transformation and become leaders themselves. These self-aware leaders form steering and action teams committed to bringing about change that creates a new climate of growth and learning for all who live and work within the organization. A new organizational structure emerges. It is designed to decentralize authority so that throughout the organization decisions are appropriately driven by the residents' desires, needs and direction. As this redesigned organization moves along the deep change progression, it designs its future physical environment, garnering necessary resources and partnerships to create a true home for the people who reside there.

This Matrix frames the transformational journey and the balance of this book. Using the Matrix, the authors will journey with you in the following pages, through the stages of change from institution to home.

Change is difficult and often times scary. As discussed earlier, we have a natural tendency to resist it. But change becomes more palatable when we can see the road ahead. It is easier to "let go" when we can see what we are embracing next. This Matrix, and the ensuing chapters are intended to be a map with signposts along the your highway of change.

NORTON SHIELDS CHANGE MATRIX
For Progression to Households

	Personal Transformation	Leadership Transformation	Organizational Change	Environmental Change
PRE-CONTEMPLATION	**Irritant Experienced** I am confronted by the fact that the way frail elders are living in institutions without home is repugnant. I hear the talk about the Household Model, but it evokes fear, anger, denial and resistance within me. "We could never do that, because..."	**I Introduce the Question** Now awakened, I pose the questions to our organization. Do frail elders, like the rest of us, have the right to home? Do they have the right to direct their own lives? Others experience initial resistence.	**We Provoke the System** Strategic planning welcomes a full review of organizational structure, environment and supporting systems. We begin the painful unlearning that brings deep change to the whole organization.	**Home or Hallway – The Debate Begins** Institutional design is challenged. The design alternatives reject institution and evoke traditional home. Initial doubt – "We can't afford it." Scarcity outlook strikes fear. Discordance experienced between household design & traditional operating model. There is no turning back. We must transform organization and operations as well as environment. Feasibility inquiry is formalized.
CONTEMPLATION	**The Internal Voice Awakens** "I wish we could, but I don't see how..." Confusion & misconceptions abound as traditional indoctrination continues to battle with the awakening voice.	**The Quest Begins** Formal and informal leaders agree to form a Steering Team committed to the quest. We Invite all stakeholders to align and participate around the developing vision	**Embrace Emerging Chaos** Our vision drives our plan. We design for decentralization of authority, departments, and traditional operating systems. We design for emerging culture of shared leadership and active learning. Impatience occurs as we perceive nothing is happening, while in fact, valuable advance-ment is being made.	**Alignment of Vision and Resources Begin** Abundance thinking begins to question scarcity outlook. Pre-feasibilities (market, financial) indicate project viability. Architectural renderings create enthusiasm and a sense of possibility. All indicators are a go. Alignment spurs us forward in investigation and further financial investment.
PREPARATION	**Epiphany results in Moral Clarity** "I must do this..." The epiphany is: The way elders live must change. I must change. Moral clarity trumps traditional indoctrination.	**We Must, But How...** We seek knowledge through study, to accomplish shared vision, values and strategies. We as leaders bring resources instead of authority.	**We Develop As Chaos Climaxes** We develop the systems changes required for decentralization i.e dining, housekeeping, nursing, activities of daily life, laundry, HR, budget. We design and develop organizational structure and culture.	**Engage Partners in Design** We conduct pre-feasibility studies. We Engage architect and other development partners, finance, design and build. Our vision, grounded in the principles of the Household Model, anchors development team.

	I Speak Out	We Commit & Resolve	We Implement the Change, Energized Chaos Erupts	Move In
ACTION	In a private confession or a public declaration, perhaps with anxiety but with clarity of purpose, I say, "I must and I will..." I confess that I must change how I lead, how I serve. I can no longer remain who I've been.	We gather all stakeholders, elders included, in resolve to change to resident-directed lifestyle thru self-led teams in a household setting. We are aligned in action.	We decentralize authority through formation of self-led teams in future households. Decision-making transitions into the hands of elders and future household members. We decentralize systems throughout the organization.	Residents move into their new home. Self-led teams move into place within and in support of home. Initial chaos is characterized by excitement, joy, and fear Residents and self led teams form relational bonds as they build home together. Individual, leadership, organizational and environmental transformations solidly integrate. Behaviors, environment, and furnishings evict institutionalism.

	I Become	We Align	The Organization Becomes Ever Learning	Home
MAINTENANCE (SUSTAINABILITY)	I evolve past the zeal of conversion to wanting everyone to be a leader. Elders must have home and direct their own lives. I will embrace this as the context of my relationship with elders and caregivers. I will commit to serve toward that end. I commit to making leaders of everyone. **I am a new leader.**	Now resolved we will align assets and resources of the organization around the vision. We are ready to redesign organizational systems, environment and structure. **We are now team.**	Organizational culture and character self-perpetuate the upward spiral of discovery, learning, adjustment and renewal. Continual cohabitation with creative chaos becomes the desired norm. **The organization becomes ever learning.**	A sense of family, purpose, and belonging is felt by those who live and work In the households Initial furnishings become adjusted to fit residents' culture and personality in their home. Personalization creates unique character in each house. Because of transformational experience, organization ratifies commitment to "never go back" by continued systemic adjustments as needed to sustain and deepen the model. Formal commitment is made to protect and preserve. Envelope of home seals in lifestyle, food, aromas, sounds, and relationships. Ongoing discoveries resulting from integration continues to deepen culture and sense of well-being Customs, rituals, and daily routines evolve and clearly reflect those who live there. **We are now home.**

Stories for Sharing

We've mentioned the power of story throughout the book. Here are some of our favorites from some of our own experiences as well as others who have made the moving journey to the Household Model including, Annie Peace, Michael Anderson, Shari Brown and Roger Beins.

Use these stories for your own inspiration, but more importantly share them with the team in various stages of your own journey as you find appropriate.

A Self-Led Team in Action

Jerrie was a bath-aide for many years in the nursing home before the organization transformed to the Household Model. I used to wonder how she could stand being in that steamy little room with no natural light day after day, year after year. But I never had the nerve to ask her.

What I knew was, residents loved to have Jerrie give them baths. Jerrie took such care with them, and despite her full schedule, she helped them completely relax and realize the full potential of a hot, luxurious bath. Amidst the hustle-bustle of the place, it was the one time they were served with total focus on their individuality. It was a 15-minute escape, three times a week. Above all, Jerrie had a heart as big as Texas, was gentle as a lamb and loved each one of them. And they knew it.

When we gathered residents to share the vision about creating a true home where they could direct their own lives within small communities, they were silent at first. I think the idea was just too big and they didn't believe it anyway. We began to ask how they would like awakening when they wanted in the morning. Would they like to eat what they want for breakfast when they want it? As we began to have specific conversations about what resident-directed service would mean, they began to come alive with a collective sense of possibilities. It was exciting to watch them become engaged in ways we hadn't seen before.

One comment we heard from the beginning was, "All this is great, but we want to make sure Jerrie still gives us our baths."

When self-led teams were organized to staff the houses, household coordinators were selected based on their leadership potential and their personal attributes. Credentials and letters after names didn't weigh as heavily. We looked for people who had a natural sense of service to others, a deep commitment to the vision and those we serve, and the ability to grow. While we ensured all the necessary skills and disciplines were present in each house, teams were assembled based on who the members wanted to work with and serve. Residents moved into houses based on whom they wanted for neighbors and with which staff members they wanted to share life.

It was no surprise Jerrie was encouraged by her peers to be a household coordinator.

Before we moved into the houses, some individuals resisted the idea of "blended roles," which means everybody helps with whatever needs to be done, depending on their licensure limit. In other words, everybody pitches in to prepare breakfast, clean house and serve residents' needs and desires as they occur. People could not picture how it would be and were afraid of the unknown. And all of us were struggling to overcome the indoctrination of how we should think and act within our specific disciplines.

Some only wanted to do what they were already trained to do: "I'm a nurse aide, if I wanted to be a housekeeper I would have applied for a housekeeper job," or "I'm a social worker, I didn't get all this training just to wipe tables," or "I like to cook, but I'm uncomfortable with the idea of giving personal care."

Education was provided to the teams on the front end and throughout the startup period in the houses. All teams were trained in servant leadership, conflict resolution, learning circles, PersonFirst™, teambuilding, critical thinking, listening, empathy and decision-making.

Once we moved to the Household Model, our fear and discomfort quickly began to recede. We began to understand it wasn't about what our jobs were, but more about living and working together like a family. We knew whom to turn to for a specific skill in any given situation, but we quickly learned it truly was about creating a home. We needed to align with each other like a family to keep it strong. Households became loyal to their own family, yet understood we all were neighbors. Resistance to blended roles was replaced by the comfort that comes with being a good, strong team member within the household family.

With time, the household teams became increasingly adept at hiring, coaching, peer evaluation, terminations, self-scheduling, budget management and more. We were proud of ourselves for being able to cook breakfast to order from 7 to 10:30 a.m.

As the administrator, I was gratified to see people who for years had been assigned daily routines begin to blossom as leaders. We had poured a lot of energy into developing household teams and ensuring decisions were made in the most appropriate place by the most appropriate people rather than by a hierarchy and then handed down through departmental silos. The power must rest with the residents and those closest in service to them. The rest of us needed to view everything we did as a resource towards that end.

I didn't realize how well it was working until I had a casual conversation with Jerrie in the car one day. We were driving down the highway on the way to an out-of-town meeting when Jerrie asked me, "You know what we are starting on Thursday?"

"No, what?"

"Twenty-four hour dining, whatever you want to eat whenever you want to eat it." She said it as casually as if saying, "I think I'll go get a cup of coffee."

I thought to myself, "She knoweth not what she sayeth." First of all, to do that, the house would have to bring in quite a number of outside resources. The CFO would have to be highly involved. The chef and central kitchen would have to be integral to it, and that, itself, would be bigger than any of us could chew. Besides, I didn't know a thing about it, and I was the administrator. Something like that couldn't happen without my knowing it. There was no way to have "24-hour dining, whatever you want to eat whenever you want to eat it" starting Thursday. She must be talking about snack plates, I thought.

I didn't want to hurt her feelings by saying, "No, heh heh, you're not really going to do that." I was starting to worry they might try to do it on their own in the house. What a mess that would be! When administrators have silent thoughts in situations like this they say what I then said, "Hmm, tell me more about that."

"Well," Jerrie said, "we've been having some weight loss in the house that we haven't been able to figure out."

"Yes, I've been concerned about that," I said, trying to sound intelligent and administrator-like.

"Well, you know, with everybody getting up when they want, we figured we needed to do something about breakfast hours."

"Absolutely," I said, thinking, "Is this leading to 24- hour dining?" Like every administrator, I wanted a one-line answer that would put me at ease. We could get to the details later.

"I mean, Bob gets up at 5:30 a.m., Eileen usually gets up about 5:45."

She began naming everybody in the house, including Dale who usually arises between 11 a.m. and 1 p.m. And Doc, who is awake for three days, and then sleeps for three days. (The surveyors had a cow with that one until they figured out our hard work to help him establish his own equilibrium was on target.)

"Yeah?" I was starting to see her line of thinking.

"Dale keeps missing breakfast and ends up having lunch for breakfast. He's losing weight."

"Uh-huh."

"So, we're going to have 24-hour dining, whatever you want whenever you want it."

"Right. So, how did you go about organizing this?" I was starting to get more nervous because I was thinking they are going to start something – I wasn't sure what – on Thursday.

"We've been doing learning circles on weight loss and that's when the 24-hour thing came up. So we invited Gail (the CFO) and David (the chef and kitchen manager) into the circle, told them the problem and what we want to do about it, and they helped us. We start on Thursday."

"Whatever they want, whenever they want it?"

"Whatever they want, whenever they want it."

My thought was so loud I was afraid she'd hear; "Holy cow!"

"You know what we're starting at the beginning of next payroll?" asked Jerrie.

"WHAT?!"

"We're doing away with shifts."

Silence.

"Tell me more about that."

"Well, when you think about it, we don't really need them."

"No, I don't suppose we do," I said (all the while thinking the last time I checked the entire health system in America was built on shifts.)

"We didn't really set out to get rid of them, but it kind of ended up that way."

"I see. Well, how does it work?" This wasn't one of those questions an administrator asks when he or she already knows the answer. I wasn't trying to get buy-in here. In fact, I felt a little like I had been bought.

"Well, Bob gets up at 5:30..." she began naming everybody and their wake-up patterns again. "We started wondering why we all arrive at work at 6:30 a.m. when we don't need everybody right then. But later in the day, we need more people than are scheduled. So, we thought if we organize around the rhythms of the residents, we can make sure we have everybody we need when need them, but not before we need them. It starts on Monday."

I don't remember much about the rest of the conversation because my head was swirling. I admit my first reaction was to feel a little stung because I didn't know anything about either issue. And then I thought, "Well, what have you been wanting for all this time, big boy?"

Everybody on the household team was driven by our shared values, and the decisions had been made where and by whom they were supposed to be made. The household team sought out resources and the resource bearers did their job. So, what is the problem?

There was no problem. At that moment, I was the problem. The reality sunk in and I almost started dancing in the car seat. Had I been involved, I would only have screwed it up and the changes would never have happened. I probably would have killed it by asking for a "Critical Pathway Checklist."

Plus, if there was any doubt whether "they" could do it…well, I was put in my place. Nailed to the wall. It's not that "they" can't do it. It's really that "we" can't.

The truth is, when "we" and "they" become "us" and align around a common purpose, great things happen. Jerrie and her self-led team broke through two barriers that 99.99 percent of health care executives in America couldn't pull off.

Now we're talkin'.

Camping with Friends

One morning some residents in the house decided they wanted to take a van ride through the state park. So eight of them and some of us who serve in the house hopped in the bus and headed for the lake. As we drove by campsites, Ruth said she and her husband used to camp at the lake all the time. She told stories about her sons bringing their friends and how they were all such good boys. Ruth reflectively told us camping was the only way her husband could get away from his job. Her eyes brightened as she described how she would have the camper packed and everything ready to go when he got home.

As we drove through the state park, Ruth looked at a grove by the spillway and said, "See those trees over there? I could sit in a lawn chair in the shade and read a book all day."

So, I asked if anyone would like to go camping. Surprisingly, five of the eight said, yes!

After a wonderful ride on a beautiful day, we headed home. As soon as we arrived and unloaded the bus, I could hardly wait to tell Annie, a team member, "I've got good news! The residents want to go camping!"

Word quickly spread, and we had a plan in no time. The residents prepared a dinner menu including hot dogs, chips, beer and s'mores, and a traditional breakfast lineup of bacon, eggs, toast, milk and coffee. We all got busy collecting sleeping bags and the necessary items. We reserved cabins at the state park, groceries were packed and off we went.

After settling into the cabins, we built a campfire. We roasted hot dogs and cooked baked beans in an iron skillet on the fire and finished the meal off with s'mores. It felt so good just sitting around the fire, eating and joking around. And it felt even better seeing how relaxed and happy the residents were just shootin' the breeze while the fire crackled.

About the time the last s'more was gone, Mother Nature surprised us with a nice shower and we all hurried to the cabins to settle in for the evening. With the rain playing its song on the tin roof, we told stories (even a few ghost stories) from our bunks until, one-by-one, the residents drifted off to sleep.

The next morning over bacon, eggs and much needed coffee, we all talked about how much fun we had the night before. It didn't feel like people feel when living in an institution for the aged. And it didn't feel like people feel who work there. It felt like what it was: leaving home for an overnight camping trip with people you love, roasting hot dogs and telling bedtime stories with rain gently pelting a tin roof.

Just like Ruth remembered.

Chronicle of a Day

Wilma is an early riser. She loves to get up around 6 a.m. and greet the sunrise with a cup of black coffee. Wilma worked hard all her life, and at age 92 does not plan on stopping, despite a diagnosis of Alzheimer's disease. She has a piece of toast and starts folding the dishtowels to be used today.

Bobbie, the household LPN, is finishing up her work for the day and comes to say goodbye. Wilma stops folding to make Bobbie a cup of coffee and toast for them to enjoy together before Bobbie leaves.

Wilma raised six children and finds special pleasure in taking care of others. As other elders and staff drift in, she gets them coffee or a warm sweet roll from the kitchen. As soon as they finish, Wilma slips in to clean up after them and sets a place for the next person.

Later, Joanie, a household team member, invites Wilma to go with her to pick up party supplies for the wine and cheese party on Friday. They hop in the car and head to the discount store. They find party trays, cheese and crackers and a few other goodies, and then stop by the liquor store for wine. They have invited the household next door to the party this week, so they choose a variety of wines plus a couple of known favorites. Shopping has taken a lot of the day so it's a quick trip through a fast-food restaurant before going home.

Back home, Wilma finds time to relax on the sofa and put her feet up while watching *Wheel of Fortune*. She LOVES *Wheel of Fortune*. Danielle, a homemaker on the team, brings her a bowl of chicken noodle soup and a ham and cheese sandwich to enjoy during her show. Afterwards, Jenny, another team member, gently strokes Wilma's arm and offers to help her to her room and tuck her in for the night.

One Nurse's Story

I began working in nursing homes in 1978. I was a 16-year-old junior in high school. Choosing this path wasn't so much a calling as a way for me to work inside without having to wash dishes or flip hamburgers. At the time I had no idea what I was getting myself into, but I never left. Serving institutionalized elders has been the sole focus of my career for the last 26 years.

I remember very clearly my first exposure to nursing homes. The administrator was a young minister, a real "up and comer" in the organization. I was impressed that he took time to show me around after hiring me. After all, he was the big boss and I was just a kid.

As we walked from the administrative offices down the hall to the nursing home section, I noticed a distinct change in the atmosphere. The lobby was very comfortable with soft chairs and low music. It was nicely decorated and soothing to the senses. The nurses' station, on the other hand, was like a war zone. People were rushing around, buzzers were buzzing and phones were ringing. Charts were flying around. Several who lived there were clustered around the desk, but no one was paying any attention to them. If I had thought then that this was a glimpse of the rest of my career, I think I would have run away and never looked back. But I didn't.

Initially, I thought it strange the man taking me around didn't seem to notice some people were tied into their wheelchairs, but I was just a kid, and this guy obviously knew what was going on. I quickly realized this was the way it was. We had to tie old people to their chairs to keep them from falling out. Almost immediately, I also began not to notice.

After only a few months of practice I was the best restraint tier in the building. Nobody could get out of my Boy Scout knots. I took pride in that. I was a good nurse's aide. I spent the next seven years doing this and other things to people I cared for because it was standard practice. We did not know any better. I hope you understand I didn't love these people any less because I woke them at 5 a.m., tied them to chairs and lined them up in the dining room. Twenty-six years later I remember many of their names and all their faces. What they taught me continues to serve me today.

Mary Ann was an independent woman. Never mind she was living with dementia. She knew very well what she wanted: to be cut loose from her vest restraint. Several times a day she beckoned me to her chair and whispered conspiratorially, "Hey mister, do you have a knife? I need to get out of here."

Then I would kneel beside her, take her hand in both of mine and say very gently, "Mary Ann, you know I can't do that. I'll get in trouble."

Then she would kick me in the shin and grin. I grinned, too. The sparkle in her eyes told me she would never give up. I silently cheered her ability to retain that little piece of personhood in the midst of an institution designed to take it away. She was a strong woman and a good friend. She taught me a lot.

Unfortunately, not everybody had the strength to keep up the fight. Most quickly grew weary of the struggle and succumbed to the will of the institution with its routines and procedures. People who had raised families, survived wars and a great depression no longer decided when to get up in the morning, what to wear or when to bathe. Of course this made our jobs easier. Compliant residents are much easier to manage. When we lined them up outside the dining room an hour or two before breakfast, they stayed put.

Then OBRA came along in 1987. We stopped tying people down. It was a good thing, but it didn't come about without a struggle. We never thought we could keep people safe without restraints, but we learned. We changed. OBRA was the beginning of changes now sweeping the country, but at the time we didn't know that. It just seemed like another government plan to make our lives harder.

I was an LPN by then, but I still worked pretty closely with the residents. I wasn't getting them up and dressed at 5 a.m. anymore because that was the aides' job. I admit, however, I did wake people up to give them sleeping medication. I knew it didn't make sense, but it was expected. I had to follow doctor's orders.

I was efficient. Right after breakfast I made sure everyone who had treatment was back in bed so I could finish early. I had a checklist of tasks, and mine was usually completed before the other nurses got theirs done. Don't get me wrong. I still cared deeply for the residents, but my measure was whether or not I got my work done. Nurses are busy people and I had a lot to do.

I was rewarded for efficiency. After several years as the charge LPN on the day shift, my employer offered me a scholarship to complete my RN training. As soon as I graduated, I was promoted to Director of Nursing. I felt I had finally arrived! I had plans, and they were going to be carried out. I was efficient and upcoming.

After awhile as Director of Nursing, I realized I had no time to work directly with residents. I had meetings to attend and policies to write. I had budgets to balance and staffing schedules to keep. Nursing ratios and quality indicators became my world. It didn't take long to realize this was not why I became a nurse.

Fortunately, through a merger I was about to become associated with an organization that was embarking on a mission to change the way elders are served and forced to live in long-term care. In 2001, after years of planning and learning we began the hard work of transforming our culture from a traditional nursing home to the Household Model. We began creating true home founded on the principles of resident directed service by self-led teams in household communities supported by values-driven, resource bearing leadership.

It has been a struggle. If you are embarking on a similar journey, don't kid yourself into thinking it won't be. But don't think for a minute this is a flavor-of-the-day fad, either. If you live through deep transformation like we have, you'll know there is no turning back.

The nursing staff I mentor is not penalized for spending time in the backyard visiting elders. If we see a household team member sharing a cup of coffee with a resident at the kitchen table, we smile and our hearts are warmed with the knowledge that our real purpose is being served. Nurses are not excluded from participating in celebrations and the life of the household--we don't agree with the notion that it is too costly for an RN to be part of it all.

I cook breakfast in one of our healthcare households every Tuesday because some of the elders think I make good omelets. They view me as a whole person rather than as just an administrative presence in their lives. Ask any housekeeper or cook: People share their feelings with those who make their breakfast or straighten their room a lot more than they do with those who make policies.

Though we are far from perfect, the staff I work with is blessed with the opportunity to be nurses in what I consider to be the profession's most pure and holistic form. We have the opportunity to engage with elders on a deeply personal level and help them live their lives the way they want.

As Clinical Services Mentor, my accountabilities are the same as when I was Director of Nursing, but my focus has radically changed. Instead of just teaching clinical services, implementing policies and coaching staff, I listen to elders and model person-first behaviors to other nurses and household team members. I help instill values of respect, caring and trust in our staff. We encourage one another to develop relationships with household residents rather than warn against getting too attached.

Beth, a young LPN, has developed a strong relationship with an elder, Emily, that goes well beyond what is considered "professional" in a traditional facility.

Emily is intensely private, rarely leaves her room and typically resists help with her hygienic needs. Beth is the only person Emily wants to assist her with bathing. They have a standing arrangement that (1) on the days Emily has chosen for her bath, they go to the spa room, and (2) the next day Beth brings fried chicken that they share for lunch in Emily's room. Emily has severe arthritis with intractable pain that is not always well controlled. Beth lies with Emily in bed, comforting her until the pain subsides. I believe this is the art of nursing at its finest.

In the end, this type of organizational and personal transformation isn't for everyone. If you need to have control over staff, or if you feel you know how people should live and need to exert your influence so they comply, this probably isn't for you. If you are reluctant to share information and decision-making authority with others, you may want to stay in a more structured institution (while they still exist). There is nothing wrong with that.

But for me and my co-workers, there is no going back after having worked through our feelings and fears, observed the simple beauty of people being themselves regardless of their limitations, and seen wonderful things happen when the administration begins changing and encouraging everyone else to take a step forward.

As for me, I will never tie another Posey. I will never again subscribe to institutional regimentation, and I will never be just a Director of Nursing.

Joe

We often picture older gentlemen as kind, little old men in fedoras shuffling down the hall with a cane. Joe did not fit the picture. He was a retired farmer, construction worker and maintenance man who could cuss fifty ways from Sunday and not feel a bit bad about it.

Joe was also a husband and father, and his relationship with his daughter Sarah was very special. Sarah had a special empathy for the pain and suffering her father was experiencing from colon cancer and Alzheimer's disease because she, too, was dying.

One Friday afternoon we received a call from the hospital. Sarah was not very strong and had missed visits to her dad's household; could he possibly come over to see her? Joe was very excited about going. I helped him put on his best shirt and hat, and we set off for the hospital. We didn't talk much on the way. He knew Sarah was sick, but I am not sure how much of her illness he understood.

Sarah smiled when he walked into the room. The social workers had called us without letting Sarah know, and it was a terrific surprise for her. She sat on the edge of the bed and talked with her dad for more than 15 minutes. As their conversation winded down I stepped back into the room. Sarah reached over and gave her dad a long hug and said, "I'll see you soon, Daddy. I love you."

Sarah died a few days later. At his family's request, no one told Joe. He continued his daily routine for a time until suddenly one evening he also died. Billie, a household team member who was with him in his last moments, described him smiling and reaching up before he relaxed and went home.

Of course, we all believe he was reaching for the hand of Sarah, his escort to heaven.

Maxine Kicks Out the Administrator

Before she was admitted to the old healthcare center, Maxine had been kicked out of at least four nursing homes over the previous seven years. She was tough as a boot and cussed like a sailor, but had a gentle, humorous and intuitive side. Her husband had been a section foreman on the railroad and she had lived in more than a few trackside houses. She told me she could make a place into home in no time.

She was no-nonsense and could tell from the start if a person was being real. If they weren't, they got the rough side of her. If they were, she was fun and kind. Either way, there was no doubt how she felt about any given subject.

She was admitted several months before we moved into the new houses. The first thing she asked when we met was, "Are you going to kick me out of here, too?"

"Not if I can help it," I said. "Why did they kick you out of the last place you were in?"

"They kept trying to make me do things I didn't want to do. What are you supposed to do, just roll over?"

I liked her immediately. "She'll probably kick me out if there's to be any kicking out," I thought. I had no idea that was exactly what would happen.

Soon after settling in, Maxine joined resident and staff learning-circle discussions about upcoming household arrangements. She heard, though didn't really believe, residents would arise in the morning when they desire and eat when and what they want for breakfast. Together, we were going to dismantle the existing system and create true homes where they would drive their own lives.

Though disbelieving at first, residents began to engage in the vision. They would get especially excited when we took hardhat tours of the new houses. They saw for themselves which house would be theirs and where their bedrooms would be.

Maxine was a veteran of the nursing home system, so it was no surprise she had the hardest time trusting the vision. "I'll believe it when I see it," she said. "I've been around the block a time or two."

Nonetheless, as we planned it out with the residents, Maxine got in her two-cents worth. It was her nature. Even if she didn't believe it, she couldn't help becoming part of it.

By the time we started moving into the houses, Maxine was charged up. She was moving into Lyle House and could hardly wait. Her daughters brought things to make her bedroom comfortable and homey, including paintings she had done years ago. On moving day, she helped decide where to place furniture, all the while being mindful of others. She made sure everybody's needs were met amidst the craziness that goes with any moving day. It was touching to watch her help others establish their home in Lyle House while she was establishing her own.

She also paid attention to everyone coming and going, carrying boxes and running every which way. I stopped in with a box of stuff for my Dad, who was moving into the same house as Maxine.

Sitting in her wheelchair, she waved me over with her one good arm and said, "I thought you said this was going to be a real house."

"It is, Maxine. Why do you ask?"

"Well, you said people would knock on the door."

"Yeah, but its moving day, so things are kind of crazy. It'll settle down. But, it is your house, Maxine. Don't hesitate to take charge if you see something you don't like."

A couple of days later somebody came to my office and said, "Maxine is throwing people out of Lyle House, and she's cussing some of them out."

"Really. What did they do?"

"Well, they need to get in to Lyle House and she won't let them."

I went straight to Lyle House. When I opened the door I heard her raspy voice before I saw her. She had parked her wheelchair where people couldn't see her if they came in uninvited.

"Damn it! Not you too!" she hollered. "Get outta here! Didn't your Mama teach you any manners!? You're supposed to know better. If you don't do it nobody will!"

I froze for a minute, turned and left the house. Then I rang the doorbell, just like we're supposed to. Behind the door I heard, "Let him wait a little bit. It won't hurt him."

I felt like a little boy who had been sent to his room. After a long minute, I rang the doorbell again. "Okay, you can come in now," she said.

I sheepishly stepped in and she gave me a glare.

"This is gonna take work, I can see that right now. What's the matter with these people? Were they born in a barn? I've had to kick out 14 people already this morning. If this keeps up I'm gonna want a paycheck."

"Why did you kick them out, Maxine?"

"Same as you, they didn't knock. Is this my house or isn't it?"

"You bet it is." I was so proud to know her I could bust. It was perfect. The context had changed from institution to home, but we weren't adapting fast enough to the new world amidst the chaos of moving in. Old habits were creeping forward and Maxine was going to make sure they didn't. She was protecting the sanctity of her home, just like we all would if ours was invaded.

"Alright then," she said, "we better all start acting like it."

"Right, I'm with you. Now, Maxine, my Dad lives here and everyone decided in learning circles that family members don't have to knock, that they are part of the household."

"Oh, that's right, I forgot. Well, if you're here to see your Dad, then come on in. If you're here on company business, then you need to knock."

"No sweat," I said. "Thanks, Maxine. I'm glad you live here." I started out the door when Maxine hollered at me. I turned back around. She was grinning like a pirate who had just found the loot.

"It feels good to be the one kicking people out for a change," she said.

Elizabeth

Elizabeth has a lot of life wisdom. She has seen sunshine and rain, known laughter, tears, life and death. What endears her to all of us is the way she embraces it all. She told me once she never thought she would find anything as important as her children. Then she had grandchildren!

Elizabeth's best days, which are frequent, are those she spends with her family. If you really want to make her smile, find a way to bring her granddaughter, Logan, over to bake cookies in the afternoon. Logan and Nana will whip up a batch of cookies, curl up with a book, a plate of cookies and two tall glasses of milk and spend the afternoon reading.

"I never thought it could be this good," she whispered to me one day.

"Having grandkids?" I asked.

"No, living here. I never thought my family would like to come visit me here. That is one of the main reasons I didn't want to move here. But did you know that Logan told her kindergarten class that her Nana has over a hundred rooms in her house? She loves to come here, and I love having her!"

Elma

Elma is a night owl. Her typical day does not begin until about 11 a.m. Cynthia ritually tiptoes into her room with a cup of hot chocolate lathered with whipped cream, and three molasses cookies. Elma stirs as Cynthia sits on the edge of the bed. They both giggle and shout out a page number. They are reading the same John Grisham book and both stay up until all hours of the night trying to be the first to finish it.

Elma is a retired librarian from the local university where she met Cynthia in the stacks more than 20 years ago. Cynthia came to work here not long after, and Elma was one of the first elders to move into independent living when it opened. Elma was secretary of the organization's board of trustees for many years.

Elma talks of the changes she has seen over the years and what it was like before we adopted the Household Model. "It has always been a good place. The people have always been kind. But I didn't want to ever end up in the nursing home. I had friends who did. I was afraid living in the nursing home wouldn't be like my home. And you know what? It isn't; it's better. Now I am not alone and I have someone to talk with about my books. And you can't live without that!"

Our House

Mealtime in our household offers a richness of ritual, camaraderie and nurturing, allowing the deepest pleasures of communal life. There's a chatter that begins to build before mealtimes as residents and staff help each other. Mrs. Johnson oversees the table-setting almost every day. When she's feeling up to it, she set the napkins out. Other days she sits in her chair and gently reminds the staff where the glasses and silver should be placed. She's a funny lady - says she should have been a stand-up comic. Shortly after she came to our household she offered a funny commentary on the proper way to set the table. Everyone enjoyed the banter and a few younger staff say they are now using her methods to set their tables at home.

The house somehow decided, no one can remember who or how, to offer a drink in the living room before the evening meal. While only a few choose an alcoholic beverage, there is a spirit of good humor and grace as we all anticipate the meal. A Homemaker will make a humorous remark: "I'd much rather be in there with you guys, but nooooo, I have to slave over the hot stove" Mr. Bigelow usually retorts with something like, "I put in a long hard day at the office. I deserve this."

The house feels especially honored to have Reverend Bennett living here as he has always been a well-known figure in our town. He had a stroke and is difficult to understand, but the blessing he utters to open the meal is appreciated by all. Mr. Williams is kinda grumpy when he's helped to the table. We know it hurts him that he has to have help with eating but once the meal gets going, he joins everyone else in enjoying the food and conversation.

We've talked about how we all have had to consciously work at slowing down at mealtime. It started with a household learning circle many months ago. The question was: "What was dinner time like at your house?" The residents talked about how mealtime was an event not to be missed. They mentioned how they enjoyed having the whole family sit down together and talk about their day. Mrs. Jacobson said she loved sitting over the dirty dishes at the end of the meal. "Just because the food's gone doesn't mean the conversation is over!"

When the staff shared about our mealtimes we talked about fast food and 15-minute recipes so everyone in our families could quickly eat and get to other things. Well, hearing the residents' stories just made us all a little jealous. Because it's the residents' home everyone (residents and staff) agreed in our household, mealtimes would be pleasant experiences not just a time to get food in our bodies.

The biggest struggle for staff was to let go of seeing mealtime as a task. It was hard to engage residents and enjoy ourselves at first. "It felt fake," Letisha recalled. "But the more we did it, the more we liked it! It almost feels like an extra break now. I especially like coffee that we have right after. Most people choose to have coffee at their table with a dessert, but Mr. Robbins always says 'let's take it to the living room!' He always finds two or three folks to join him. I like helping make that happen, and when I can, I sit for a minute and have a cup too."

We still may have hurried take-out dinners at home sometimes. But here, in our household, meals are always something to look forward to. The food is great, but the company is a treat.

chapter 7
Personal Transformation

"Whatever you can do, or dream you can, begin it. Boldness has genius, power, and magic in it."
- Johann Wolfgang von Goethe

PERSONAL

Irritant Experienced

Internal Voice Awakens

Epiphany

I Speak Out

I Become

This chapter and the balance of the book takes you through the Matrix.

IRRITANT EXPERIENCED

You know you're in pre-contemplation when...

You have worked in long-term care long enough to be aware of the sense of loneliness and homelessness in your organization. You see elders unhappy and tuning out. You think, "Boy, I'm glad that's not my mom…or me." But then you think, "It's too bad. But I can't do anything about it." You try to ignore it. Still, your thoughts nag you and the situation turns your stomach a bit.

Have you ever noticed how dust builds up without our seeing it? We go about our days without giving the furniture a second look. Everything is fine. And then we get a phone call from an old friend. She's in town and can she stop by? As we say, "Yes! Of course!" we suddenly notice a thick layer of dust covering the bookshelf and coffee table. Tiny spider webs cling to the lampshade and dust bunnies crouch in the corners.

"When did that happen?" we ask ourselves, "I'm sure that was not there this morning." Of course, we know the dust has been building up all along, but not until our friend calls does it draw our attention. Otherwise, it likely would have continued to build.

It happens all the time in our organizations as we prepare for survey. No matter how vigilant we've been, as survey time approaches we begin seeing clutter in the hall and serious problems with the charts. Suddenly everything weighs more heavily on us.

Problems generally go unnoticed, sometimes for a long while, because facing them is hard. We are busy. Solving problems and making lasting change takes time, energy and strength—resources that are nearly tapped out just by dealing with life's day-to-day tasks. We may know a situation is problematic, but we deny that it really needs our attention. In the meantime, the problem becomes more deep-seated the longer it goes unaddressed.

It's Not a New Problem

It is common to realize residing in a long-term care facility is not a desired way to live out our days. We all fear ending up in a nursing home, yet for the most part we continue to let the ones we work in function as little more than warehouses for frail elders. We may provide exceptional nursing care, but the implied promise of "home" in our nursing home is all but ignored.

"We may know a situation is problematic, but we deny that it really needs our attention. In the meantime, the problem becomes more deep-seated the longer it goes unaddressed."

Home allows us to find our little place in the world, take it into our hearts and make it our own. We are drawn to our kitchens for a favorite snack to comfort us, or to prepare a meal to share with friends and family. We relax with TV, books or conversation in the living room. We rest better in our own bed than anywhere else. We may even have our own special space like a sewing room, study or lazy chair where we can be alone with our thoughts.

These amenities are what distinguish "shelter" from "home." Despite its excellent clinical care, a traditional facility without an emphasis on the qualities of home holds no more comfort or identity for its residents than a doctor's office, library or hotel. We may visit these places often yet have no emotional attachment to them. Moving the furniture or talking informally with other patrons – let alone taking personal ownership of the surroundings – isn't something most of us would even consider.

While visiting a facility in Michigan's upper peninsula, I met a woman who expressed her discomfort about living in a place that did not feel like home.

"It's not just the large size," she told me, "I was raised among 17 children. My mom would buy a bolt of cloth and all of us girls would end up with the same dress for Easter. I hated it. But, that was nothing compared to institutional life here. We loved each other. We looked out for each other. We were wild and had fun. We sat around and had great times together. You never knew what would happen on a Sunday afternoon! But here, even with all these people, I am so lonely."

Try on a pair of catalyst glasses that allow you to see the dust, the problems. Let yourself see the degree to which your facility honors home, normalcy, relationships, privacy and choice. Walk through your facility with new eyes and play a game – "Things That Are Stupid" or "Things That Are Not Home" or "Things That Would Make Me Crazy If I Lived Here." Do it not because you can change these things immediately, but because you need to see. We need to experience the irritant as the first step to changing it.

Do you see these things?
- No salt and pepper shakers or sugar packets on the tables.
- Lists that dictate when people take baths; elders pushed in

"Despite its excellent clinical care, a traditional facility without an emphasis on the qualities of home holds no more comfort or identity for its residents than a doctor's office, library or hotel."

"We need to experience the irritant as the first step to changing it."

wheelchairs down the public hallway to the bathing room, naked under their robes, feeling vulnerable and cold; the dreaded shower chair experience.

- Schedules for awakening residents, starting at 5:30 a.m. when you dress them and set them in front of the nurses' station to snooze for two hours until breakfast.

- Residents put to bed at 6:30 p.m.

- Waking residents up every two hours to turn them.

- The facility turned into a prison for fear of elopement.

- Alarms placed on the bodies of confused residents that go off every time they get up. What must that feel like for the elder? Does she become increasingly anxious about the alarms yet unable to escape them to somewhere that feels safe?

- No real "alone time" for residents, especially for those paired with a stranger for a roommate after having lived for decades alone or with a spouse. Nowhere for the resident to go for quiet and solitude.

I once visited a lovely, recently renovated facility. Included in the renovation was a fenced-in yard costing $150,000. The door was opposite the nurses' station. I started to go out but the door was locked.

"Why do you keep the door locked if the yard is fenced in?" I asked.

"Oh, we can't have residents coming and going without supervision. Someone might fall," was the reply.

"How often do people actually get to use the yard?" I asked.

"Well, the Activities Department takes people out sometimes. We use it for our Fourth of July barbeque and the administrator had a party for the residents last month."

Later that same day, I spoke with a resident who had lived her entire 87 years on a farm until she moved to the nursing home. I wondered, but didn't ask, if she missed the outdoors.

It Won't Resolve Itself

You recognize that current operating systems do not honor the residents' need for home. You may find the realization overwhelming and think, "This is how it has always been done. Who am I to think there's a better way?"

You may bury it subconsciously so you don't have to face it. You have a job to do, so you become callous to the elders' homelessness so you can continue working without distraction. Still, you have begun to awaken. You hear talk of the "Household Model" or "culture change," but it evokes fear, anger, denial and resistance in you.

You think, "We could never do that because___," or "People will think I am foolish to say such a wild thing," or "That might work for facilities with assisted living, but our residents are too frail," or "Residents don't stay here long enough," or "Residents don't want 'home' here, they tell us they want to go to *their* home."

These thoughts and feelings don't mean you won't move forward in your transformation. As with any change or journey, there is trepidation, especially at the onset. We can't help being attached to what we know.

As you begin to break down your resistance to seeing the problem and recognizing change is needed, you begin moving from pre-contemplation to the contemplation stage.

There is resistance but also intrigue. We've all seen the old movie where the leading lady tells her leading man, "I despise you," yet she is drawn into his embrace. He has stirred something so strong inside her it scares her. She wants to forget about him but can't. That makes for some serious inner struggle *and* chemistry.

Everybody resists change. When we finally quit resisting it feels good to be out of those shackles. But resistance is quickly replaced by confusion. And then, confusion increases.

"Yeah. Ok. I need to change but HOW?! What do I do now?"

You want to hide. You want to find someone to help you. You might feel scared. You may even try desperately to forget what you have seen with your new eyes.

Listening to the Inner Voice

But the inner voice that calls us to this work – the little voice shoved aside by our indoctrination – knows the simple truth of it all; that people should not have to live as they do in nursing homes, and that we do not want to live like that when we become old and frail.

Our inner voice is the key to creating deep, lasting change, but heeding it after ignoring it for so long can be painful. Few of us can easily accept that what we are doing is wrong. We rationalize to feel okay about it.

"As with any change or journey, there is trepidation, especially at the onset. We can't help being attached to what we know."

When we collectively cause something bad to exist and finally can no longer tolerate it, we commonly find a sacrificial lamb--somebody or something else to blame. Thus we divorce ourselves of accountability and ease our collective conscience.

If cause and effect isn't direct, (i.e., if we can not see how our role in perpetrating an unnatural and inhumane system contributes to Lee Chung Hi's screaming), it is easy to avoid feeling accountable. Indirect cause and effect is no less powerful (or destructive) than an obvious direct relationship, but it is easier to hide from.

If we honestly listen to our inner voice, we will hear that we individually are integral to the system. Every single one of us is part of the problem—and part of the solution. To change the system, we must first change ourselves. Doing so involves much painful unlearning and a deep commitment to understanding the ugly truth about our current nursing home culture

We can get past internal resistance by letting the quiet voice inside dominate our head, heart and soul. In time, the quiet voice grows into a roar too loud to ignore. That's when fear transforms into thrill.

There is a fine line between "scared" and "thrilled." Being scared is paralyzing. Being thrilled…well, it means you are on your way. The harness on the roller coaster has been buckled. There is new-car smell in your nose. The rapids splash your face. There's an engagement ring on your finger. You get the point.

As people, we are comfortable and familiar with walking around this Earth. We do it all the time. We *know* how to walk so well we rarely think about the ground beneath our feet. In fact, being land-bound creatures might not even come into our consciousness until we are 10,000 feet up in the air looking out the door of an airplane and getting ready to jump. Super heroes, angels and Santa Claus are special to us because they fly. We long to be "free as a bird." But the chance to personally fly is scary. Then, somehow the line between scared and thrilled is crossed and we can jump from the plane. Things will never be the same. The feeling of "thrill" we get is nature's little boost to help us risk what we *know* for something that can be so much better.

"The feeling of 'thrill' we get is nature's little boost to help us risk what we know for something that can be so much better."

"When you realize things can be better and you start to dream about the possibilities, thrill sets in…feelings of burnout are replaced by the joy of feeling so very alive."

When you realize things can be better and you start to dream about the possibilities, thrill sets in. It's so tantalizing to have something new, hopeful and radical in your life. It is like falling in love. You can't stop thinking about it. You read up and search for more information. Your feelings of burnout are replaced by the joy of feeling so very alive. This excitement builds the bridge to the next stage. It, like the adorable factor with puppies and children, will help you through tough times.

THE INTERNAL VOICE AWAKENS

So you've jumped out of the plane and no matter how hard you wish it, that's not going to change. You will never go back to being ignorant about our elders' homelessness. But, wow! Now you are falling through the air and you feel you have no control. Your mantra has changed from "It won't work" to "I wish it would work, but I don't see how it can."

The contemplation stage is marked by confusion, questions and misconceptions. It's a time of weighing in. You think about why things are the way they are. Who decided it should be this way? Is it the regulations? Is it the owner of the facility? Is it some long gone DON? Is it the elders? And you know honestly it is *not* the elders.

So now you know the way-things-are is not the way that honors and nurtures elders. You can't *not* see it. You walk down the halls of your nursing home and can no longer ignore the slumping and calling out. You notice the institutional clutter and the sounds in the dining room. Suddenly it is so loud you want to scream.

Ambivalence continues to haunt you. You go through your assumptions: You are the only person who feels this way. Your opinion and ideas don't matter. The powers that be would never allow change. There is no other way of operating.

Your optimistic voice answers: But there *has* to be a better way. Those other facilities changed.

You feel the momentum gathering in your mind. You look up "culture change" on the Internet, go to a presentation and have a conversation with someone who has gone through it. You start to look for the rip chord on your parachute.

PERSONAL
Irritant Experienced
Internal Voice Awakens
Epiphany
I Speak Out
I Become

Leaving the Comfort Zone

One reason we resist change is that it means having to leave our comfort zone. That's pretty basic and most of us know that. But, what we often don't see is that our comfort zone is only a familiar zone. In reality, it does not hold much comfort at all.

Oddly, in organizations that have a resistant or negative culture, leaders join followers in resisting change. The resistant energy is so strong that leaders succumb to the will of the masses. Leaders and followers feed

"Oddly, in organizations that have a resistant or negative culture, leaders join followers in resisting change."

off each other's resistance until it is the only accepted culture.

As a leader, you have to lift yourself above the fray, find your will and acknowledge your primary responsibility to lead and encourage change. If you set yourself apart to lead rather than to resist, you will encourage others to find their will.

We like to think being in our "comfort zone" is easy and relaxing and makes us content the way comfort should. However, staying in a comfort zone that no longer serves us is a lot of work. Everything is changing always. Standing against the wave is much harder than floating with it. We could spend all day blocking out signs of progress around us; simply close our eyes, ears and minds to new ways of thinking and doing.

Organizational change is often stifled because we feel there is not enough time to do what change requires. The organization does not want to divert time away from its primary tasks into having discussions and training that could grow the organization and its employees. But extra time and energy is spent on resisting change anyway, so why not put it to better use.

So let's go there. Let's contemplate what could be changed, what could be possible. It might sound a little like this:

"Is it possible to do something? Can *I* do something? What have others done? The front lobby where all the residents gather in their chairs for hours – couldn't we do something to make it friendlier? Maybe have magazines or free coffee. What if we met with the receptionist and helped her figure out some things she could do with the residents. The activity room – It's such a great room. It has a stove, refrigerator and cabinets. But we only use it for activities. Why can't we do more with it? I wonder if a small group of residents could have their breakfast there. Maybe residents who are able to get there on their own could form a breakfast club. We'd need supervision. I don't see how we could manage that. I don't know if the state would let us do it. The residents deserve their own rooms. But that would never happen."

You may find yourself talking to residents differently. You want to know how they lived before. What did they like to do every day? How did they do meals? What time did they get up? Did they eat breakfast in their pajamas? What did they have for breakfast? You'll hear stories like we have:

Mrs. Johnson laughed about her cold pizza habit. She said she would order pizza in the evening with no intention of having it for supper. She

"We like to think being in our 'comfort zone' is easy and relaxing and makes us content the way comfort should. However, staying in a comfort zone that no longer serves us is a lot of work."

would immediately put it in the refrigerator when it arrived. She'd have the first slice the next morning for breakfast and another for lunch.

Mr. Ransom talked about his life as a farmer. He'd be up at 4:30 a.m. and have coffee and a biscuit or two. Then go out in the fields until 7:30 a.m. when he'd come in for breakfast. He liked two sandwiches and a thermos of coffee for lunch, which he'd take with him to the fields. He'd have a big supper and then a piece of cake or a bowl of ice cream before bed. Now, he only eats three meals a day rather than five, and he rarely sees the outdoors except through his bedroom window. But don't worry about him. He can adjust to anything . . . even this, he said grimly.

Mr. Brown's morning habits included lying in bed and listening for the newspaper to hit the porch. He lived life in anticipation, he chuckled. He'd scoot out the front door barefoot no matter how cold it was. He'd have a cup of coffee with the paper. It often took him an hour to read everything. His wife would have *Good Morning America* on in the family room, but he called that "pop" news. He always folded one page carefully to the crossword puzzle and set it aside for evening. He'd done that his whole life, but now his eyes weren't so good. His son grew up wanting to do the puzzle, too. He'd find his son's penciled words in the boxes, but he always finished the puzzle in ink. He was that sure of his answers. And now, his son always brought a crossword puzzle to work on while he visited.

New Tools

There are many tools and resources to help us through life. In our garages or workshops at home we may have a half-dozen Phillips-head screwdrivers. But, chances are we have one or two that we consistently reach for even though many are available to us. And, if somebody gives us a new one as a gift, chances are it will end up in the pile with the others. We still reach for our favorites even if they aren't the best size for the job at hand.

We all do this. We rely on a few favorite methods for every occasion even if they are not the most effective. (Those methods are in cahoots with the comfort zone.) It's time to dust off some tools that have made their way to the bottom of the tool case, or even discover what new and inventive tools are out there. (See "Living and Working In Harmony" workbook for

LWH inspiration.)

"We all do this. We rely on a few favorite methods for every occasion even if they are not the most effective."

PERSONAL

Irritant Experienced

Internal Voice Awakens

Epiphany

I Speak Out

I Become

 Our personal characteristics dictate the speed with which we journey through the contemplation stage. You will want to address these points:

- How do I always deal with change? Do I fear it? Roll with it? Embrace it? Go after it? How does it affect my mood? Be aware of this and know the difference between honest reactions to a new situation and reacting to a situation because it is new. Prepare by being aware.

- What do I believe about my own abilities? What are my strengths and weaknesses? Which strengths will help me here? What weaknesses do I need to overcome?

- What needs do I have with regard to approval and acceptance from others? Do I rely on it? Do I not care what others think? What degree of acceptance am I willing to deal with? It's fine if they think I'm crazy, but I don't want to get fired.

- What is my ability to consciously navigate through self-awareness? Am I willing to look at myself honestly? Can I ask myself the hard questions?

- What is my history and confidence as a trendsetter? Am I comfortable going out on my own? Do I like to lead or to be led?

- What is my positional authority and its inherent risks? Who and what am I responsible for? What am I risking in terms of career? What could I gain?

- How strong is my personal support system? Do I have people at home who will support me? At work? Other friends?

Change is both an internal and external journey. Throughout the transformation you must continuously and closely monitor changes going on inside of you and in the environment around you. Consistently evaluate progress on both levels to ensure they are in accord.

"Change is both an internal and external journey. Throughout the transformation you must continuously and closely monitor changes going on inside of you and in the environment around you."

"It is not enough to merely do no harm to elders…You must also honor them."

EPIPHANY BRINGS MORAL CLARITY

It is not enough to merely do no harm to elders. That is a given. You must also honor them. If you pass by someone hurt on the street and do nothing, you have further harmed that person. You have a responsibility to change the system. You can no longer carry on the status quo. *This* is your epiphany. You have examined your beliefs and listened to your inner voice, and now you know the truth. The way elders live *must* change and you must help make that happen. Your mantra becomes, "I must do this." You find you are in control of your own change and you pull the ripcord.

I became CEO of Meadowlark Hills in 1994. One of the first things I did after beginning my work was to get my mom out of the horrible nursing home she had been in for four years and move her to the healthcare center on the Meadowlark campus. During those four years our family had watched in disbelief as Mom declined into someone we hardly recognized.

Mom lived at Meadowlark Hills for the next five years. We were all relieved at the high quality of care she received. She dressed in her real clothes, got her hair styled and wore make up. As much as possible, she looked her old self. Meadowlark Hills was deficiency-free on state and federal surveys year after year. We were proud of what and who we were.

Mom began to quickly lose ground in late Spring of 1999. By early June, it was evident she was dying. In the last five days of her life, I stepped out of my role as Executive Director and became a full time son. Dad and I were at her bedside almost constantly. We did our best, along with a very caring staff, to make her comfortable. She had been a dancer and a classical pianist, so we played Chopin softly in her room.

Being a family member in residence made me experience our healthcare center in a new way. Everybody was so kind but always in a hurry. I lost track of all the different staff members who came into her room to do single, focused tasks. It didn't feel good to me, yet I appreciated each person's efforts.

After several days of keeping vigil, we were exhausted. It really took it out of us to watch her labor to breathe and lose ground by the hour. Neither Dad nor I said it aloud, but we wanted her to go peacefully, not the next day, but right then. It was painful seeing her suffer.

I needed to get out of the room for a few minutes so I walked to the nursing station, set my elbows at the end of the counter and cradled my face in my hands. I didn't realize it, but my life was about to change.

As I rested, I lost myself. I heard nothing, felt nothing. I was somewhere else for who knows how long. Then slowly the unrelenting bustle of the nurses' station returned me to the present. Ear-piercing beeps, clacking carts, telephone conversations and hallway-chatter—the kaleidoscope of noise muffled frail voices calling for assistance. Although I had been surrounded by these sounds daily for five years, suddenly I heard them. As I raised my head and looked around, I saw everything as if for the first time.

People in uniforms rushed from place to place, nobody spoke to the people who lived there. Residents slumped in chairs around the nurses' station. The sights and sounds played before me like an out-of-tune orchestra with the strings snapping on their instruments.

"This is crazy," I thought. "What are we doing here? The system makes people run around like chickens with their heads cut off doing everything but building relationships with the people who live here. We've got to stop this!"

Sanctioned madness was preying on every nursing home in America, and as CEO I was perpetuating it.

From that moment forward, I had new eyes. Everything about how I felt, what I saw, how I reacted was different. I could not continue with the status quo. Even as Mom lay dying, I became acutely aware that my new charge was to be a catalyst for change, rather than be in charge of a deeply flawed system. It was a powerful epiphany for me.

Prochaska says in his book, *Changing for Good*, "Preparation takes you from the decisions you make in the contemplation stage to the specific steps you take to solve the problem during the action stage."

Basically, this is game plan time. You realize you must change, no matter what. At this point, change is not something superficially pleasant like painting a room a different color. Change is a moral choice.

Changing From the Inside

Personal change, the kind of deep transformation we are talking about, is not just about actions. It is about attitude. It is about how you see yourself and others. In his book, *Building the Bridge As You Walk On It*, Robert E. Quinn talks about the normal and fundamental states of leadership.

In the normal state, he says, we are self-focused, internally closed, externally directed and comfort centered. In the fundamental state, we are other-focused, internally driven, externally open and purpose centered.

Most of us, regardless of what industry we work in, are in the normal state of leadership most of the time. A person in this state thinks primarily of job responsibilities, happiness and comfort. She is not seeking solutions to problems, nor does she see her role in them. She continues to do what she has always done.

"You realize you must change, no matter what. At this point, change is not something superficially pleasant like painting a room a different color. Change is a moral choice."

In the fundamental state of leadership, she thinks first of the elders. She is driven by her desire to have meaning and purpose in her life by bringing meaning and purpose to the lives of the elders. She is open to opportunities, possibilities and insights from those around her. She honors the person first.

In your own situation you know there is a lot within you that must change. You suddenly feel inadequate to the task. How can you see so clearly yet act the same as always, or at best, merely stumble at change?

"I Must Do This."

The absolute realization you must somehow change leaves you weak in the knees, anxious and fearful of failure. You may or may not be in a formal leadership position in the organization's hierarchy. Either way you doubt your leadership skills. This is the time to address that fear.

Take a good look at what scares you. You don't have to overcome it on the spot. It is a process. But really think about your fears. Know them well. Anticipate when they are likely to surface and the effect they might have on you. You must make a conscious decision that fear will be a useful tool but that it will not drive your actions. Fears can be dealt with. It helps, however, to know our weaknesses and what to expect. Without the element of surprise, fear loses strength that we in turn gain.

Next, it is time for a pep talk. Cut off that internal negative voice before it gets too loud. Have you ever seen a boxer just before a fight muttering to himself? He's getting ready. He's getting pumped up. He's speaking his mantra.

You have to know *your* mantra – "I **must** do this." You must, you want to and you will.

You may already have checked out the exits in case of emergency. You may have an "Oh, never mind!" speech prepared or someone in mind to hand the torch to when things get too tough. You could set yourself up to be defeated by roadblocks. "Well, if I mention it in a meeting and so-and-so and what's-his-name think it is a bad idea, I'll drop it."

Cut off your exits, commit to your cause and set your sights forward. There will be more doubts and fear in this journey. We won't kid you. But it is time to start practicing your defenses.

Self-Awareness

We are all born with self-awareness that we can further develop

"Cut off your exits, commit to your cause and set your sights forward."

to guide our behavior and achieve our true potential. It starts small, of course. As babies we quickly learn if we cry we will be fed. So, we apply crying to other discomforts, like wet diapers, and learn it works there as well. It starts with Mom, who in the beginning is barely distinguishable from ourselves. In time, we apply these same tactics to Dad and other caregivers. As babies, our involvement in the world is pretty basic. We are hungry and that makes us uncomfortable. We cry. We are comforted and fed. It mostly boils down to food, diapers, illness and emotional support on very basic levels.

As we grow, our thinking, emotions, wants and needs become more complex, as does the self-awareness process. We observe the situation and take in data. We use the data to assess the situation and what it means for us. Our assessment causes our feelings about the situation to arise. Our thinking and feelings help us form intentions, and from there we act.

The Spiral of Learning

The Spiral of Learning is an evolution we move through not only in our daily lives, but also on a grander scale in our culture. Similar cycles are the framework for the Scientific Method in scientific discovery, the Learning Cycle in formal education and the Leveling Cycle in psychology. We start with raw data that we process into conclusion, action and behavior. For the most part, this process comes naturally. We do it many times a day and don't even think about it. Sometimes we skip the thinking part or blow through it quickly and let emotions dictate our actions. We also run into problems when we don't take time to get all the information, our thinking is flawed or we don't act.

By taking time to purposefully move through the Spiral of Learning, we improve our chances for a positive, productive outcome. Your new thinking will rejuvenate the learning process, enabling you to grow in new ways that enhance your leadership and contribute to the growth of others as well.

Spiral of Learning

1. Observations	4. Intentions
2. Interpretations	5. Actions
3. Emotions	

"By taking time to purposefully move through the Spiral of Learning, we improve our chances for a positive, productive outcome."

For example, you observe that the lawn is overgrown. It is your son's chore to cut it. You think, "Maybe he has been too busy with school and activities to have time to do it." Or, you think, "I have repeatedly asked him to cut the lawn and he has ignored me and gone out with his friends." Maybe you feel sympathy because he is so busy. Or, maybe you're angry that he didn't do what you asked and ignored you. You can decide to cut the grass for him. Or, you can leave it and wait for him to notice how overgrown the lawn is. Or, when he returns home you can tell him he can't go anywhere until he mows the lawn. Then, you act on one of those intentions.

In culture change it is important to stop and commit to self-awareness. The conscious sense of self is vital because with the change in culture comes change in data, thinking, feelings and intentions. Your awareness of how these changes impact your interpretations and emotions will enable you to make the transition in culture as effective and smooth as possible. Keeping tabs on your internal thought processes also will give you a sense of stability and control to help alleviate the feelings of anxiety that accompany change.

The Spiral of Learning techniques can help you break through self-imposed barriers to self-awareness. Ask yourself the following questions and honestly assess your behavior and the effect these issues have on your self-awareness.

- Am I blaming others and avoiding taking responsibility for my role in the situation?
- Is my outlook clouding my judgment?
- Have I articulated my values and goals and used them as a measuring stick for my behaviors and actions?
- Am I too tentative or too imposing; afraid to take action or squelching others?
- Am I seeing myself as others see me?

Practice the Spiral of Learning as you address these questions. What is the raw data? What do you think about it? What is the situation? How does it make you feel? What will you do about it? How will you do it?

Your Moral Clarity Trumps Traditional Indoctrination

The good news is, confusion and ambivalence turns to clarity and you see everything differently. Intellectually and emotionally you can no longer perpetuate the traditional model of care. Still, you continue to do so everyday. You simultaneously feel obligated to make something happen yet incapable of doing so. The struggle is no longer with *your* beliefs and values. It is with the-way-things-are. You have stopped letting the current drag you along. Everybody else is going about doing things the way they always have and you pause to compose yourself before swimming upstream.

You know that you alone can't change the system. You have to get folks to swim in the same direction as you. This does not mean you pick the direction for everybody else or that they do your bidding. Directing others to go in your direction won't work. You know this challenge can't be "managed." Somehow you have to lead. Leadership is helping others do the right thing; they will not *follow* you. You must somehow stir in them what has been stirred in you, and then ask them to *join* you in working together for change.

You must lead by example. It's cliché, but many things are cliché because they are true. It is human nature to mirror what confronts us to some degree. When someone is hostile to us, we can get flustered and feel hostile right back. When someone treats us with kindness we are likely to respond in kind.

When you go through personal transformation, don't be surprised if people behave differently around you. When we ourselves change, we change how people see us. Before you know it, you'll be leading without even thinking about it. Leadership will naturally follow your transformation.

Mahatma Gandhi said, "We must become the change we want to see."

We cannot change others. We can only inspire them. Gandhi inspired and did grand, great things we may never equal. But that small quote, those nine words, can move us to become better people. That may not seem like much compared to how Gandhi led millions, but at this stage in your journey, it means everything.

You decide – even if you don't know how and even if the goal proves nearly impossible – you must proceed. There no longer is a choice. You begin to think, "If I can't make this happen, I will have to leave this facility and find one consistent with my values, as I can no longer perpetuate this."

You've been called to give meaning and purpose to the lives of elders, and doing this will give meaning and purpose to your life as well. You know what you must do. You have a game plan: You will help every person in the organization go through the same transformation that is well established in change theory. You will band together with others and begin to transform the organization. The final outcome will be a transformed environment where elders live and create their home.

"Leadership is helping others do the right thing; they will not follow you. You must somehow stir in them what has been stirred in you, and then ask them to join you in working together for change."

"We cannot change others. We can only inspire them."

I SPEAK OUT

The parachute opens and you settle in for the ride. It is time to privately commit to and publicly declare your intentions. Declaring your newfound beliefs will help anchor you in them so you are less likely to slide back into old ways. The spoken mantra is, "I must and I will..." Like an addict who wants to change, you have to look squarely at old habits and begin to think and act differently. If you don't model it, you won't become it.

Modeling the Change

With the declaration, you acknowledge *you* must change. You're not saying, "Ok, everybody else should do x, y and z." You are aware change begins inside you. Your change will be a model for others, giving them a clearer path for joining in the journey.

It may feel a bit awkward at first. When we have done something the same way for a long time we often don't realize we are doing it. Imagine your morning routine: Shower, brush your teeth, dry your hair, get dressed, get the paper, look through the front section and then the sports, grab a mug of coffee, kiss the family goodbye, get in the car...

Have you ever arrived at work and thought, "How did I get here?"

Chances are your morning routine is the same every day in every detail. It's habit. You do it without thinking. Now, let's say you are going to start going to the gym and eating a healthier breakfast. You will have to wake up earlier. You take your shower at the gym instead of at home. You eat some fruit and cereal before you leave instead of stopping for a raspberry jelly doughnut on your way to work.

You will have to fight the urge to stay in bed, and remember to take clothes and toiletries with you to the gym. You will have to say goodbye to the baker who always had your donut and a weather update waiting for you. You will have to think about what you are doing because it all is new and not yet habit.

Let's say you're a charge nurse on D-Floor West. You normally punch the clock and then get report. You always tune in when the third shift nurse tells about the clinical change of conditions. You review the paperwork and make a note to check on the more serious changes immediately. You review the other changes as you pass out meds. You may say, "Hello" to the CNAs in passing, and you definitely will speak with the aide who is caring for the resident in need of extra vigilance today.

PERSONAL
Irritant Experienced
Internal Voice Awakens
Epiphany
I Speak Out
I Become

"If you don't model it, you won't become it."

PERSONAL

Irritant Experienced

Internal Voice Awakens

Epiphany

I Speak Out

I Become

But then you think, "What about the other residents and CNAs?"

You need to pay attention to them all, but how? It's such an overwhelming thought. You decide to start small with one strategic, person-centered change. You decide to always ask the third shift nurse which resident isn't doing real well today, who doesn't seem happy and who might just need a few minutes of your time to help them have a good day.

Keep the ball rolling by constantly evaluating and monitoring how your actions are changing, perhaps by keeping a journal or sending yourself a daily email. This helps you work things out in your head and provides a written record so you can look back and see how far you've come. Talk about your feelings, struggles, accomplishments and plans. You can keep it to yourself or support your peers' journey by sharing it with them at a team meeting or in a learning circle.

Start With Small Ripples to Make Big Waves

You cannot change what is outside of you without changing what is inside. However, once you change the inside, changing the outside goes from being a desire to becoming a necessity. You change from being a believer in change to becoming a leader of change. This is how others will begin to change, too. You model your change by what you see, do and say. You point out the elders' need for home. You share culture change literature. You take time with residents, do with them instead of for them; ask them instead of tell them. The things you say and do--the conscious choices of a self-changer--are symbolic, substantive models to guide others.

Speaking out is a pivotal point. You suggest the journey, lay out the map and call others to action.

I BECOME A LEADER

You have landed on the ground safely and are elated. "Wow! I feel fantastic!!" you say. Those who have been watching...well, they want to do it now too. You testify to your experience with enthusiasm and commit to making leaders of everyone.

You stand on the knowledge that elders must have home and direct their own lives. This knowledge will motivate your every action. It will be the context of your relationship with elders and caregivers. You will commit to serve toward that end.

"You cannot change what is outside of you without changing what is inside."

"You change from being a believer in change to becoming a leader of change."

Facing Barriers

It takes courage to continually identify and confront self-imposed barriers. Fear, insecurity and the draw of that which is comfortable are never gone for good. You've reached the point of no return but that does not mean the path is obstacle-free. Of course, the more you encounter these barriers, the better you get at overcoming them.

The institutional barriers also will get in your way. The hierarchical structure of the organization has a well-worn path for information and responsibility. The new structure will need new paths. The current culture may be traditional, patriarchal and hierarchical. Things are done the way they have always been done. The organization is not one for risk or change. There is a protective, father-knows-best tone to procedures and care.

You may be willing and ready to do your job in a new way. However, that does not mean everybody else is going to like it, or even that you will know how. Everything you do must become person-centered. How else can residents be acknowledged and direct their own lives? Organizational and departmental practices will be tested as priorities begin revolving around people rather than the institution. You will also have to confront traditions and staffing structures that discourage personal relationships.

Make It Contagious

Obviously, this is too much to take on by yourself, so now you commit to making leaders of everyone else in the organization.

It was at this very point that a small group of staff at Pennybyrn at Maryfield in High Point, NC, including the CEO and Administrator, began realizing the need for change in their nursing home. As Eden Alternative Associates, they could see things no one else could. So, they invited others to train and become Eden Associates until they were a group of ten. They met every two weeks. "Did you see that? What should we do?" they asked one another.

As this little group with new eyes (and moral clarity) struggled with how to change their organization, they realized enormous work lay ahead. Though it appeared daunting, no one wanted to turn back. Their first challenge was to get others to join them in demanding change.

chapter 8
Leadership Transformation

"Some go first, and others come long afterward.
God blesses both and all in the line,
And replaces what has been consumed,
And provides for those who work the soil of helpfulness."
- Jelaluddin Rumi

I INTRODUCE THE QUESTION TO OTHERS

Transformational change never starts with everybody at once. There is usually one person or small group who initially questions the status quo – who is first to begin informal conversations of unrest and/or excitement about a possible new way to do things.

As a new leader, your first act is to introduce the question to others. These new ideas are entrancing. Momentum builds until it becomes clear it is time to take the revolution to the next level.

Silence is no longer an option. Once an individual's awareness rises to this level, there is little choice but to begin disturbing the system. It is time to round up the cavalry – to look around and see who is willing and able to struggle through their own leadership transformation and lead this change with you.

 Just as you have attended to your own self-awareness, it is now time to help others grow theirs. Begin by using the Spiral of Learning and ask these questions of your colleagues to lead them through the process.

- Observation – What do you see? Hear? Taste? Touch?
- Interpretation – What do you think about it? What does it mean? What do you think it means? What does it mean to you?
- Feelings – How do you feel about it?
- Intentions – What do you intend to do?
- Actions – How will you do it? What did you do?

You can help each other by periodically bringing up these questions in one-to-one conversations, or at group gatherings to increase everyone's *shared* understanding. The learning circle provides the perfect vehicle for group discussion.

"It is time to round up the cavalry – to look around and see who is willing and able to struggle through their own leadership transformation and lead this change with you."

"In a learning circle, no person's voice holds more value than another."

Learning Circle

When people gather, they naturally do so in a circle. When someone new comes along, someone says, "Hey, pull up a chair!" and everyone moves a bit, creating a larger circle to make room for the new person. Not only is a circle the most conducive form for stimulating conversation within a group, but it is also a form within which no point has greater value than another.

In a learning circle, no person's voice holds more value than another. Everyone is heard as equals, which builds a sense of respect and team. Each participant is given the opportunity to speak without being interrupted or judged. The learning circle draws out shy people and encourages those who are more talkative to listen. Everyone has a chance to examine their own views and those of other circle members, leading to broadened perspectives and a wider base from which to build relationships and discover solutions.

2 Eight to fifteen participants sit in a circle without tables or other obstructions blocking their view of one another. One person is chosen as a facilitator to pose questions to members of the circle, give encouragement and keep the responses moving. After posing the question or issue, the facilitator asks for a volunteer to respond with his or her thoughts on the chosen topic. A person sitting beside the first respondent goes next, followed one-by-one around the circle until everyone has an opportunity to speak on the subject without interruption.

Cross talk is not allowed. (However, staff should help draw residents out with cues and acknowledgement.) One may choose to pass rather than speak when it's his or her turn. But after everyone else in the circle has had their turn, the facilitator goes back to those who passed and allows them another opportunity to respond. Only then is the floor open for general discussion.

Whether to solve hard-core problems or simply help people get to know one another socially, learning circles are effective for addressing a wide variety of topics – even among individuals with very limited cognitive abilities. Use learning circles as part of regularly scheduled meetings or as a handy tool for dealing with issues as they come up. In the circle, ask questions about observations, thoughts, feelings, intentions and actions. This helps everyone grow in self-awareness, group cohesion and critical thinking.

Learning Circle Steps:
- Facilitator poses question
- A volunteer goes first
- Work around the circle
- No cross talk
- Second chance for those who passed
- Open for general discussion

You Can't Do It Without the Executive Leader

The stirrings for change and the desire to change the way elders live may begin at any given place in the organization, or with any given person or group of people. The power of energy for change coming from within the organization can be a wonderful thing in terms of momentum and organizational drive. But, in the end, if the head of the organization is not part of that drive, or leading it, then the potential for deep change is substantially mitigated. The Household Model, with its complexities and requirements of profound transformation, cannot come to fruition and meet its full potential without the executive leader.

When the CEO leads the process from the beginning, doors open much more quickly for everyone in the organization. If the CEO isn't the initial driver, those who are stirring for change must invite him or her into the dialogue. If, at the beginning, the CEO isn't receptive or "doesn't get it," be persistent about bringing him or her to a point of understanding. This isn't easy. Culturally we are accustomed to stopping after the first try when we are met with resistance from our bosses. But, don't give up. Remember your obligation to the elders and let that obligation help you overcome your hesitancy.

Had Annie Peace not been persistent with me at Meadowlark, we would not have been fortunate enough to find the right people to help us learn about (and eventually become a partner in deepening and refining) the Household Model. In 1997 Annie was my administrative assistant. Annie was invaluable to the organization and me as we struggled to articulate and plan for deep change in our organization. I knew we had to do something different, but I didn't have the language to truly help guide the organization in a new, clear direction. At that point, we were still struggling with our identity as an organization. We knew we wanted Meadowlark to be home, and we had decided to let go of institutional trappings, but we didn't know much else. The words "culture change" were not known then. Nothing had been written about it that we knew of. We were struggling, thinking we were alone.

Annie and a couple of others suggested that we go to PersonFirst™ training in Kansas City. We were in the middle of an expansion and I felt I was just too busy to go. (We CEO's tend to feel that way a lot.) So they went without me. When they came back I was "too busy" to ask her how it went. But she told me anyway.

She said, "Steve, you need to meet these people—Megan Hannon and LaVrene Norton. I think they have the answers to some of the questions we are struggling with."

I said, "Oh, that's good. I'm glad you went." I had never been so busy and I went about the day trying to keep up with the pace that I had been setting around the building.

A couple of days later Annie said, "I have the number for you to call LaVrene Norton."

"Who?"

"LaVrene Norton. I told you about her the other day. I think you need to call her."

"Yeah, okay. Set it on my desk."

Several days later Annie asked me, "Did you call LaVrene?"

"No, I haven't been able to get to it."

She got up, walked over to my desk and said, "Do you trust me?"

That stopped me. "Of course I trust you, Annie. Why would you ask me that?"

"Because you aren't listening to me. You need to call LaVrene Norton." She handed me the phone and looked me in the eye. I knew she wasn't leaving my desk until I made the call.

That call was a very important one to say the least. Had Annie not pushed me to move toward something (or someone) that I didn't think I really needed, then our story would have been a very different one. Elders at Meadowlark would not be living the life they are living today, tomorrow, or ten years from now. And LaVrene and I would not have even met, let alone written this book. (So if you don't like it, you can blame Annie.)

So please, don't give up.

We also see many instances where CEOs will designate a "Culture Change Coordinator" to make changes in the organization happen, but not change themselves in the process. They treat deep change like a program rather than a comprehensive and complete organizational transformation. The head of the organization must *become* the change desired rather than delegating the change to others. If not, everybody will bump up against a ceiling in their efforts to grow change.

If the head of the organization does not transparently model the change, including all of his or her personal struggles to do so, others in the organization will not have full license to transparently struggle themselves. In addition, the administrator or CEO is instrumental in orchestrating all of the support systems that must transform in order for the Household Model to reach its full potential. If this doesn't happen, at best it will be a limited but heartfelt effort on the part of only a segment of the organization.

We see this in its most glaring form when chains or multi-site systems pilot deep change in one site, rather than starting first with their core at the corporate office. The facility will earnestly create change to the degree that they are able, and regional managers will make their regular site sweeps using their traditional style of top-down management. One site administrator told us, "We work so hard between her visits, but after she leaves I have to spend two weeks getting everybody picked back up after she lets the air out of everybody's tires. I can't see being able to truly transform here if corporate methodologies and systems aren't consistent with what they expect from us. Its like they want a trophy out of this, but don't want to run the race themselves."

What Is Leadership?

Leadership is about character, not position. In the past, leaders have seen their role as strong-faced decision makers. We all have believed that is what we need from a leader. He or she must stand up stalwartly and give direction to the rest, who then follow.

One of the authors knew a CEO who carried a small, dog-eared paperback published in the early 70s – his "Bible," he said confidentially. It said leaders are born, not made, and most people in the world are followers who are weak and confused. They don't want to be leaders, only to be led. The born leader, elevated in adulthood to management, is obligated to do just that. He (we doubt there was a "she" in the book) must take up the pain and difficulties of leading and insist the followers do as he says. Where the leader goes, the followers gratefully (even while grumbling) follow.

The book's premise is laughable, but we all have residue of this attitude within us. We look to the leader for direction. Or worse, stand around and wait for him or her to fail. We watch and critique his or her fumbling, detached as if watching a TV drama unfold.

We, in turn, do our best to guide those who follow *us*. We worry ourselves sick over our decisions and pass on our expectations to subordinates. When we become aware that they, too, watch and critique *us*, we wonder why they don't appreciate all we do for them.

In contrast, the transformational leader is more of a guide than a king. This leader does not say, "Go forth and bring back that which I ask of you," but shares leadership, saying, "Please come down this path with me and let's see what we can discover together." This leader grows other leaders, who, in turn, grow others. Followers do not serve the leader. The leader serves the followers.

As you move from thinking of yourself as a manager to seeing yourself as a leader, you may feel some of the responsibility and accountability is taken off your shoulders by sharing leadership with others. In truth, everyone has *more* responsibility and accountability.

A leader cannot hide behind rules, regulations, institutional culture

"Leadership is about character, not position."

and the-way-things-are-done mindset when setting and enforcing expectations. As a leader, part of your service to the followers (those who follow you on the path to their own leadership) is being personally accountable for your leadership actions. You are responsible not only for the ends but also the means.

Shared leadership leaves no room for blame. The new leadership model distributes not only power, but also accountability. From now on you will all, *together*, enjoy the victories and confront the obstacles and setbacks.

Awareness Brings Light to the Path

As a new leader your eyes and mind are open. You are aware. This does not mean that because your flashlight is on you won't run into tigers. No. It means now you'll be able to see the tiger. If you couldn't see it and didn't know it was there, you wouldn't be afraid. But it still could attack and you wouldn't know what hit you. Now that you see the tiger you must find the courage to address it and every other animal that crosses your path.

By being open and aware you can collect a very good cross-section of data. This new data does not reflect assumptions by which you previously operated. Now, you know new places – and ways – to look. You are no longer limited by the myopic vision of the traditional model. You strive to keep your vision clear and you listen more than you tell. Once you get the hang of this, the gift of foresight follows. You begin to anticipate a bit, while remaining open to *all* possibilities. You count on there being unknowns, but are prepared to deal with them.

Information and awareness of how to use it properly will help you look to the future. That is why we need leaders – not to take us where we've been or to keep us in place but to help us traverse the unknown.

If you plan to move from the traditional model of care to the social model, *everyone* in the facility must eventually make the journey. As the saying goes, "You can lead a horse to water but you can't make him drink." As a leader, you need to help others recognize their thirst so they will walk with you to the pond. Once they know where the water is, they can show others the way. Being a leader is not about demonstrating your power, it is about teaching others to realize their own power.

> "We need leaders – not to take us where we've been or to keep us in place but to help us traverse the unknown."

> "Being a leader is not about demonstrating your power, it is about teaching others to realize their own power."

Who's In?

So, who will join you? Who are you going to agitate?

Of course, invite those folks you heard whispering about culture change. Grab the person who really connects with the elders. Select somebody in administration and somebody who knows about organizational finance. There are others you might not think of right away, like the person who is always negative and complains about how things are. Ask her if she would like to see a change. She may be "negative" because she, like you, is angry about the way elders are treated and frustrated because she feels she can't do anything about it. Think how successful and vocal she is in relating her unhappiness or negative attitude. Imagine what she could do if she had a positive outlet for all that energy! Leadership must come from all levels and departments – even from people you didn't think of as "leaders."

Maybe your facility has a quiet person, a CNA, for example, who elders open up to, is very detail oriented or inspires cooperation among residents and staff. He may not be a formal leader, but he and others like him may have great, untapped leadership abilities. Find natural influencers in maintenance, dietary, bookkeeping and HR. Look beyond staff to residents, families and the community to give inspiration and to voice their special stakes in the organization. Assure all spheres of influence in the organization are reached. Get the fingers of change in every nook and cranny.

Just as you questioned yourself to heighten your awareness about the elders lives and their need for home, you must also shake up the hornet's nest and create a buzz among those around you. Ask the question, "Should elders live like this just because they are frail?"

You are not just making conversation by posing this question (though hopefully it will lead to many heated discussions). You are provoking folks into moving toward change. Follow up questions might include:

- What does "life, liberty and the pursuit of happiness" mean?
- To whom should it apply – only the young and able?
- Do we all have a right to home?
- What are the vital elements of home to you?
- Tell us about the first time you walked into a nursing home.
- What did you want to be when you grew up?
- How do you want to live when you retire?

"Get the fingers of change in every nook and cranny."

"You must shake up the hornet's nest and create a buzz among those around you. Ask the question, Should elders live like this just because they are frail?"

- What do we do and see that is not home here?
- Do elders have a right to direct their own lives?

The answers you hear likely will vary a bit. I once met a woman who, when posed with the question, "Do elders have a right to direct their own lives?" replied, "Are you kidding?! Would you let your two-year-old run her own life?"

Questions like these will make people think, and their answers will clue you to the issues and beliefs that create and perpetuate the-way-things-are. Shining a light on the oppositions will help you better address them.

Awakening Others

Posing questions is not the only way to shake things up and inspire action – there are hundreds of ways to provoke those around you. It's hard to know what makes the light go on for each individual, so try different approaches. Talk, watch videos, read, download from the Internet, drag folks to presentations, buy leadership books, pass along articles and do whatever you can think of.

Though we use the words "agitate" and "provoke" to convey the importance of being persistent and insistent, tread carefully. Remember the fear, resistance and anger you felt when first confronted with the sad reality and the need to change it. As you bring your cause to others, they may experience those emotions as well.

We couldn't say it better than do Heifetz and Linsky in their book, *Staying Alive:* "To lead people, we suggest you build structures of relationships to work the tough issues, stabling norms that make passionate disagreement permissible. But keep your hands on the temperature controls. Don't provoke people too much at any one time. Remember, your job is to orchestrate the conflict, not become it. You need to let people do the work that only they can do."

Others must change their hearts and minds before we can change our collective professional and organizational behavior. A lesson learned on your own always sticks better than one given by someone else. Like you, folks will go through their personal transformation in their own way and at their own pace.

Remember your new self, your ability to be open and confident, and your dedication to the life, liberty and pursuit of happiness for elders. Let your determination and patience reign as others join you in transformation and purpose. Perhaps most difficult of all, refrain from action on your own (except to listen to, inspire and engage others in new ways) as you garner their interest in exploring possibilities. You will gain trusted allies in the quest that will lead to team action.

THE QUEST BEGINS

You and your change companions may feel a little like Dorothy, Cowardly Lion, Scarecrow and Tin Man from *The Wizard of Oz* as you join together and are off on your journey. Both formal and informal leaders may feel clumsy and unsure, but you all know you must make your way to the Emerald City of "home." It all starts with the Steering Team.

Form the Steering Team

The Steering Team should be comprised of formal and informal leaders. At the start, all department heads should be part of the Steering Team and, of course the Administrator and/or CEO, but as the process moves on some may step out to make room for informal leaders. The Steering Team will guide Action Teams that will be established to work through various parts of the transformation process.

Together you will grow as you shape and affirm your values and share leadership. For your first meeting, get the Steering Team together to craft a value statement to guide the team's work. (See *Living and Working in Harmony.*) This can be a review and renewal of an existing value statement, or you may start from scratch.

Values should, of course, include "the right of home and choice for elders," but should also extend to how care is given, resident/staff and staff/staff relations, high involvement in decision-making and pursuit of personal growth. Keep the statement handy and refer to it often. When making decisions, your values statement will be your guide.

This is also a time to plan how the Steering Team will progress, learn more about your facility, its people and their ideas, and investigate how other facilities have made the culture change journey. Start discussing how to gather the information.

By now, you recognize a hallmark of the process of the transformation to households: questions. Each new step, hurdle and conflict starts with questions. Questions bring clarity when we're confused, ideas when we're stuck and direction when we start something new.

"The Steering Team will guide Action Teams that will be established to work through various parts of the transformation process."

"Each new step, hurdle and conflict starts with questions."

It's All About Questions

 Ask questions like these in your first Steering Team meeting:

- What kind of study shall we pursue?
- How can we, and how have others...
  - (1) Change(d) workplace culture?
  - (2) Move(d) toward resident-centered or resident-directed care?
  - (3) Increase(d) choices about bathing and dining?
  - (4) Renovate(d) into home?
  - (5) Create(d) high involvement of staff, residents and families?
- How shall we involve others in this study?
- How shall we discuss the findings?

We cannot over-emphasize the importance of involving all stakeholders in as many ways as possible, and the sooner the better. Reach out to staff, residents and family members outside the Steering Team as you begin to study and shape what you hope to create. Bring a wide variety of perspectives into the process to gain deep understanding of the desires and needs represented at the facility.

Diversity will lead to a truly shared vision. The process and outcome will belong to everyone. You are working to create a home, which not only is a physical environment but also an atmosphere. It is a place that belongs to us and a place where we belong.

While we strongly advocate researching other organizations for ideas for your own culture change journey, remember that every organization and its residents are unique, just as we are in our own homes. The only right way is the one most agreeable to the residents who live where you serve. What you see and learn elsewhere is not prescription. It is inspiration.

Asking questions, examining your values, researching other organizations -- everything you do in the study phase must be deep and far-reaching and involve as many people as profoundly as possible. Thoughtful study may take a year to complete.

So, get all stakeholders on board and visit other Household Model organizations and culture change facilities. Create small groups to research different issues and bring back information to the whole group. Look also to the Internet, books, culture change organizations and seminars. Schedule

"The only right way is the one most agreeable to the residents who live where you serve. What you see and learn elsewhere is not prescription. It is inspiration."

LEADERSHIP

Introduce

The Quest Begins

We Must...But How

We Commit & Resolve

We Align

yourselves to work on a unit to closely observe day-to-day procedures.

Evaluate the way things are. Look to quality control and human resources data, regulatory compliance, satisfaction surveys and financial indicators.

Then, again ask questions:

- What if we erased the organizational chart? How could we start over?
- How do we organize our lives at home?
- How do we feel about ourselves as a team?
- What are our strengths?
- What do we want that we don't have?
- What are we pleased about?
- What do we need that we don't have within ourselves?
- Do we need outside help?
- If we were in the residents' shoes, what would we want?

And most importantly, ask the residents what they want. Talk to residents and their families about their homes.

Sense of Team Emerges

As you study, you will learn much about the Household Model, your own organization and the people who live and work there. And, you will find the prize in the Cracker Jack box: while you've been studying, you've become a team. Team building is a byproduct of work that is occurring. You all climb into a van, drive for hours, see something that blows your mind and then spend the return journey trapped in the van, unable it seems, to talk of anything but your dreams.

WE MUST...BUT HOW?

The preparation stage of leadership transformation is all about devising a plan of attack. The Steering Team shapes itself, its current and future Action Teams, and assumes responsibility as guide for the journey. It designs the overall initiative within the context of the organization's mission and values. So, keep that values statement handy.

Using the Matrix as a guide, the Steering Team begins by mapping out each stage of the journey. This can't always be done in its entirety before beginning the journey; there are too many unknowns and too much opportunity to go in different directions within the chaos. You will need to re-route the process as it progresses.

While the specifics may change the one thing the Steering Team must do from the beginning and throughout is strive for 100 percent involvement of all stakeholders. You are striving for resident-directed decisions in every way possible. High involvement doesn't wait until move-in, it is the foundation on which every step in the journey is built. It is the most important tool in your pack.

You are encouraging leadership not only in staff, but also in residents. It is the elder leadership that will solidify and ensure deep change and rich life.

Ethel had come to the nursing home "to die." She had given away all her possessions since she did not expect to be around much longer to need them. When she moved into the facility they were living the Household Model in the original facility and soon after moved into a new building. Ethel was thrilled to have her own private room and bath. After six months her health had improved quite a bit, as did her attitude. One day, a nurse aid was in Ethel's room and saw a video cassette sitting on her table. The aid asked about the video and Ethel explained that it was her favorite movie and that she had given it away when she moved in but had recently asked for it back because, as she explained, "I'm going to live."

Ethel enjoyed crafting. She made centerpieces and scrapbooks and soon made a special bond with her next-door neighbor. Flora was not doing as well as Ethel was, so Ethel always took Flora "home" after meals in the household dining room. When it became apparent that Flora was dying, Ethel and some staff members took it upon themselves to take shifts sitting by Flora's side in her last hours. A neighbor commented, "Ethel always showed Flora the way home, now she is showing her to her final home." In the old model, an administrator observed, Ethel and the staff never would have thought to take Flora's care into their own hands like that. But now, it's just the way life is in the household."

Preparation Checklist: A general description of the process follows. Use it as a template or checklist as you proceed.

- An individual is interested in creating home.
- Based on her position, she introduces the idea into the organization.

"High involvement doesn't wait until move-in, it is the foundation on which every step in the journey is built. It is the most important tool in your pack."

- Meanwhile, she becomes a role model, grows her own leadership skills, begins to lead in new ways, stimulates interest by others and helps them develop leadership skills. They, too, begin to lead.
- Formal and informal leaders collaborate and form a Steering Team to guide the organization's journey.
- The Steering Team:
  (1) Defines and articulates the vision and excites others.
  (2) Works to define the purpose, vision, goals and actions needed.
  (3) Engages others in study.
  (4) Forms Action Teams, each with a clearly defined mission and autonomy to perform within distinct parameters identified by the team's purpose, the overall vision for change and the potential legal ramifications.
- Each team struggles with their particular short and long-term obligations over the entire course of developing households.

Action Teams Join In

The Dining Action Team, for example, studies and discovers ways to give residents choice in dining experiences. The ultimate goal is to have decentralized dining in each household, and maybe offer five meals a day or have the kitchen open 24/7. This requires several months of grand restructuring of the organization and the physical environment. In the meantime, why not introduce a continental breakfast for early risers or keep a cabinet full of residents' favorite snacks to munch anytime, day or night?

While moving toward a long-term goal, strive to find things to implement along the way. It brings motivating gratification and builds confidence and momentum. Besides, now that you understand the need for home, how can you wait any longer? Changes that can be made in the-way-things-are-done without great preparation, renovation or compliance issues should be implemented as soon as possible.

"While moving toward a long-term goal, strive to find things to implement along the way. It brings motivating gratification and builds confidence and momentum."

We, The Organization

We always think the "organization" controls the way we do things or the climate in which we live. Truth is, the organization is not some supernatural force. It is the people who comprise it. You and I are the organization. We often see this phenomenon in relation to government. We complain about "the government" and the way "they" do things. Yet, every fourth grader knows "*We*, the people" are supposed to say how the government operates.

Whether reclaiming our organizations or government, diligent study and persistent activism are required. Each and every one of us must develop our leadership skills and become highly involved to make things run the way we'd like. If you work somewhere long enough to see significant employee turnover, you'll see the organizational climate change with personnel. We're not suggesting giving everyone the boot and replacing them with culture change advocates. But rather, as the *mindsets* of the people in the organization change, so does the organization. So, at this stage it is very important to grow the concept of team. These teams will become increasingly skilled and eager to create home.

The Steering Team, which always includes the organization's senior executive, determines the resources needed, seeks and allocates them and monitors their use. It addresses macro-resource issues such as assets and property. Is there money and room for renovation? How much? Is there underused space in the facility? Where do you most need or desire to use resources? (This is addressed in more detail in Chapter Ten)

Also take stock of your talent pool. You'll find many hidden skills among staff and residents. Sue in dietary has a way with wallpaper…John in housekeeping can bake a mean cherry pie…Mr. Grant plays piano…Mrs. Roberts loves to knit--all these talents can help create an atmosphere of home.

Don't overlook opportunities to involve family and community members. Embrace the concept of investing resources to the greatest extent possible. The greater the investment in learning the greater the development of learning capabilities that boost people's enthusiasm and their commitment to the new initiative.

Finding Time

You must also consider the most critical resource – time. Beware and prepare. The further along you are in the journey, the more time the journey absorbs until move-in day. "But," you say, "everyone's usual job already takes up so much time. Where are we going to find time to meet, do research, ask questions, develop leadership skills and implement change?!"

True, long-term care is time-starved. Most of our jobs are task

"Don't overlook opportunities to involve family and community members."

"True, long-term care is time-starved."

oriented and focus on fulfilling the expectations of management and regulations. It seems there is no time to even *think* about concepts like resident-directed service or modeling new behaviors for others. Many administrators and department heads welcome involvement by informal leaders and are delighted by how effectively direct-service staff participates in team efforts. Yet, knowing *how* to involve them remains problematic because of time and staffing issues. Be prepared for this to be your first and most important challenge in achieving high involvement and shared leadership. You cannot be successful if you do not work through this issue. At some point your new team approach stops being "added time" and becomes who you are. It becomes the way you spend your time.

Some direct-service staff may not show up for team meetings, and you might become frustrated with *them*. They knew the time of the meeting. They had agreed to do this. Surely they can get "off the floor" for a few minutes. You are tired of their excuses. Time to take the big leap!

The leap you need to take is to realize this is not a personal performance problem or a sign that they don't care. It is merely a reflection of the institutional nature of your organizational structure. Not the person, but the system! As leaders, you must think through the problem and work toward systemic solutions.

Solutions to the issues of time and staff should include use of direct-service staff, but also *must* include people with check-writing authority. In other words, this problem can only be adequately resolved if you're willing to consider solutions that require an investment of staff hours from all service areas, including administrative. Consider having your Steering Team take on the resolution of the time/staff problem as its first goal. Find solutions that encourage informal leaders to participate.

Here are some solutions other teams have discovered:

- Household Model meetings are held at shift change on Tuesdays when an additional caregiver is scheduled to go from unit to unit to cover for staff attending meetings. Caregivers and dietary folks come early and/or stay over. Those who don't attend meetings but put in extra time to enable other workers to attend are compensated.

- Department heads and other formal leaders are trained as CNAs and feeding assistants so they may care for residents directly and fill in for caregivers attending meetings.

- A department head holds meetings or other activities with residents from a particular hallway to lighten the load for caregivers who are

"At some point your new team approach stops being "added time" and becomes who you are. It becomes the way you spend your time."

on duty while other workers attend team meetings.

- Meetings are held in the hall or near the wing where team member caregivers work, enabling them to be available if residents need them. Meanwhile, coworkers try to cover for caregivers attending team meetings.

- Direct-service staff members are encouraged to attend meetings on their days off and are compensated for the hours they attend. This type of incentive should be made known before attendees are recruited for various teams.

Learning As You Go

You must make time aside from your job responsibilities to learn and grow, but ultimately you must also make learning part of the job. Robert Quinn hit the nail on the head in *Building the Bridge As You Walk On It*. He wrote, "What we know from past experience is an asset, but what leads to successful transformation is our capacity to learn in real-time."

And so, leaders must learn. Literature on leadership promotes "action learning," or learning on the job. The Household Model requires everyone to learn on the job. We can't stop serving elders while we all go to school to learn how to better serve them. Instead, we must learn together with our elders in our midst.

How do we learn? The same way we've always learned. The way we learned to do addition and subtraction in grade school or play the piano. We practice over and over. We practice talking to each other in ways we've never done before. We practice listening. We practice not making the decision but conferring with the new team first. If we are strongly opinionated, we practice keeping our mouths shut while inviting others to speak. If we are quiet, we practice speaking up and stating our point of view. We seek a new balance, and we get there by practicing day after day.

Leading vs. Managing

Is it hard for a manager to model new leadership? How could it not be? Everything that made you the manager you are today is what we ask you to set aside. You're the manager because you are well spoken. We ask you, as a leader, to be quiet and let others speak and lead.

You're the manager because you look and see – analyze quickly and accurately. As a leader, you must ask others what they see.

"You must make time aside from your job responsibilities to learn and grow, but ultimately you must also make learning part of the job."

You're the manager because you are able and willing to make tough decisions. We ask you, as a leader, to give decision-making power to the team whenever possible and foster its ability to make tough choices.

You're the manager because you always seem to know the answer while appearing confident in your knowledge (whether or not you really are). We ask you, as a leader, to explore unfamiliar terrain where you don't know all the answers, and to do it publicly while maintaining your confidence that creating home for frail elders is the right thing to do.

Steering Team Becomes Initial Self-led Team

Throughout all this, the Steering Team grows into the organization's first self-led team. It must define itself, its responsibilities and how it will relate to existing managerial, clinical and departmental teams.

As your organization's pioneering self-led team, the Steering Team decides how it will grow and demonstrate a new set of team skills that all teams are expected to eventually develop.

Let the six qualities of culture change leadership guide you:
- Grow awareness in self and others.
- Inspire and motivate through story.
- Shape a vision together.
- Involve elders, their families and staff.
- Build community and create team.
- Show the way by walking the talk.

(From Action Pact Leadership Training available to download in *Free Resources* at www.actionpact.com)

The process is not always pretty, and Steering Team members must be able to tolerate the chaos, confusion, resistance, fear and anxiety that will be byproducts of all this good work. Formal leaders will be tempted to micromanage the Action Teams. The Action Teams will not spin off wildly in disarray if the Steering Team focuses on:
- Identifying vital parameters in which Action Teams work (provide choice; limits of physical renovations; within budget and regulations; and decision-making as close to the resident as possible.)

"You're the manager because you are able and willing to make tough decisions. We ask you, as a leader, to give decision-making power to the team whenever possible and foster its ability to make tough choices. "

- Providing autonomy within those parameters.
- Assuring Action Teams have resources and that all members, including hourly staff, are able to attend team meetings.
- Holding Action Teams accountable for identifying goals (within the purpose and parameters) and determining and implementing actions to achieve them.
- Freeing the Action Teams to be self-led. They will experience autonomy, satisfaction, team struggle and, ultimately, team growth. Your confidence in them will lead to more confidence in themselves.

LEADERSHIP

Introduce

The Quest Begins

We Must...But How

We Commit & Resolve

We Align

WE COMMIT AND RESOLVE

"Commit" and "resolve." There is strength in those words. You're putting your well-laid plans into action. Some or all of your team members may go through another bout of panic. The awakening leader's internal voice of vision and possibilities must kindly ask the voice of insecurity to stand at bay. The voice of insecurity has its purpose. It is our friend – a tool for self-monitoring our actions. But ultimately, your vision voice must send your insecure voice to the bleachers.

Think of your vision voice as your internal coach. Once insecurity is sent to the bleachers, Coach Vision calls your voice of courage to the playing field. Courage is nothing but controlled fear turned to action.

The Steering Team should use the following strategies to guide early work. They will build a strong foundation for confidence and progress.

Strategies: Self-led Team, High Involvement, Learning Company, Community Building With Elders

Self-Led Team Strategy:

Self-led teams have been breaking the traditional hierarchy of management in many industries for a while now. The team creates its own mission, and then plans and executes strategy to fulfill it. Team members rely on each other for support and to monitor progress and conflicts. In other industries the word "team" is sometimes used to describe, for instance, a sales department. Such a team is a group of people who may share the same goal but does not necessarily work together to achieve it. Nor do they let their shared goal shape their vision and work. They may have team spirit, but the kind of team we are talking about is much more.

A self-led team makes decisions, plans, shapes and not only does the task, but gives birth to it. Burnout occurs when jobs are unexciting, not

"The awakening leader's internal voice of vision and possibilities must kindly ask the voice of insecurity to stand at bay."

when they demand excessive effort. With little celebration, satisfaction or excitement about one's job, it is no wonder turnover rates are the norm. We rely on secret personal satisfactions--interacting with this resident or observing that moment of meaning--to keep our jobs interesting.

Self-led teams in long-term care are unique because they include the consumer. Elders are involved in their own care. They drive and direct the team. Much dissatisfaction by residents and workers comes from decisions handed down from above. They will be far more satisfied with and committed to the home and work they themselves create.

Work in long-term care is so very different than in most other services. Long-term care encompasses all the needs and desires that arise spontaneously in daily living. Obviously, this manifests itself in different ways for each individual. Household team members must make decisions about their actions and perform tasks on the spur of the moment depending on the situation, resident and day. For the most part, one-size-fits-all policies simply don't fit.

On the other hand, a fast food restaurant may serve many customers at the same time, but workers serve them all in the same way. The consumer comes to the establishment, orders from a menu (chosen by the restaurant), pays, takes the food and the transaction is complete. The time, conditions and personal investment under which the exchange occurs are restricted. The parameters are set by the management or ownership of the fast food restaurant. The customers expect no more than the quick delivery of cheap food.

In fast food, because the premise is relatively simple, every transaction is basically the same in every restaurant and company. In their corporations, it is reasonable for management to direct the operation from off-site, even from a different city than where the restaurant is located. In nursing homes, because staff serve the whole person day after day, service parameters are developed on the spot. The-way-things-are-done must be decided by the elders and those who directly serve them.

Self-led teams identify untapped or wasted energy and study how to convert it to usable energy for recapturing mission-based values. Organizational culture is defined by operative values, beliefs and habits. Attitude changes needed for transforming culture come by experiencing success. Our beliefs begin to change as we see the possibilities. It energizes us. We use the energy to perform our jobs in a manner consistent with our personal values ("I love old people," "Everyone deserves a good life," "They're just like me," "Home is central to the human community.") As the

"Self-led teams in long-term care are unique because they include the consumer. Elders are involved in their own care. They drive and direct the team."

fruits of our labor manifest, attitudes gradually change even more. New energy is released and new habits take hold. Then, bolstered by reflection, dialogue and discussion, new personal and community beliefs form.

With strategies that include blended or versatile worker roles, maintenance and dietary staff can grow their involvement in the household by receiving CNA training. CNAs can train in food safety and maintenance regulations. As job responsibilities broaden (but not necessarily increase) there is more opportunity for personal satisfaction. As workers care for the "whole resident" in a variety of ways, they become more "whole" themselves…more like a person in a household than an individual at work. That is key for creating home.

High Involvement Strategy:

Information and education alone are not enough to foster deep personal commitment and get staff to embrace culture change. You achieve far more with direct, hands-on experience. You want engagement, involvement and universal participation. Only then can you experience a true and deep change in culture.

Those involved need to personally adopt the mission as their own. People see in the vision what they want to change. You must envision, individually and as a group, what will or could transpire five or ten years out. You must envision, individually, yourselves as the consumer. Discover the whys and why-nots of the way things are and how they could be.

W. Edwards Deming's well-known 14 points for management (see www.deming.org) include:

- Create constancy of purpose.
- Remove barriers that rob hourly workers their right to pride of workmanship.
- Break down barriers between departments.
- Institute training.
- Replace quotas with leadership.
- Involve everyone.

Deming envisioned these strategies for the workplace, large or small, and for industries from manufacturing to service. Universal participation brings greater worker satisfaction and commitment, and ultimately creates a superior product or service.

Deming and other quality-improvement gurus helped American

industries transform their cultures and gain dominance in the global market during the 1980s. If their strategies stimulate worker participation in widget factories and fast food restaurants, why not among compassionate caregivers committed to creating a home for their elders? Certainly, no industry more than long-term care requires each person's contribution to be successful.

We will say it again (and again and again...), for deep change to succeed you must involve elders as much as possible as soon as possible. Organizations are usually reluctant to involve elders at the beginning. But if you do, you get the deep learning needed to form the basis of all your work.

I consulted in a facility in Colorado during the early 90s. They were in danger of getting their license removed and asked us to come in and help turn the situation around. We said we would help only if they gave 100 percent participation in the solution. We began right off the bat using learning circles that included residents, staff, family and community members. It soon became apparent everyone thought they knew how other parties felt about them – and none of it was nice!

The CNAs were sure they knew how the nurses felt about them. The nurses were sure they knew how the CNAs felt. Staff was sure how family members felt as well. Everyone operated on assumptions and profiles compiled from little incidents and narrow viewpoints. People took what little they knew about a person and based their whole opinion and attitude on it.

At one of the circles there was a resident, an old smoker, who had had a stroke and talked out of the side of her mouth. She was constantly demanding a cigarette. They limited the number of cigarettes she could have to three a day (doctor's orders?) She got them from the nurses' desk and had to have somebody accompany her while she smoked. She would go to the desk and ask for one and they would say, "No. You already had your three for the day." Even if she had had only two, they tried to put her off because they didn't have time to go and sit with her while she smoked.

The resident became furious. Everybody became a "bitch" in her mind. People passing her in the hall would say hello and she would holler, "Bitch!"

Her husband came in everyday. He was such a sweet guy. All the staff felt sorry for him. "He is such a nice guy and she is so mean."

"For deep change to succeed you must involve elders as much as possible as soon as possible. "

One day the resident and her husband came to the circle. We went around the circle and when it was her turn, she made a disparaging remark about the "stupid" group and she said she should be able to have a cigarette whenever she wanted. She thought it should be up to her. Then it was his turn.

He looked around and said, "You guys just don't get it. Three months ago she had the stroke. Up until that day, if you wanted to buy a new home, you had to go to her and she would decide whether you got the loan or not."

Everyone just sat there with mouths open. Nobody had thought of her as a person before that moment…a person with a real life. She was a loan officer at a bank. What she said and did mattered – really mattered! And now she was nothing but a thorn in their side. She had become just the mean, old smoker.

Afterward, people referred to that as the turning point when they all began to "get it." They began to "get" being resident directed – to understand it was about acknowledging the person, and that people are still people and have a right to a real life, no matter how frail or where they live.

You can't get those lessons – you can't truly study – unless you have these kinds of experiences. If you put a circle of people together and include everyone, together you will have experiences that are meaningful, poignant and significant. There will be lessons all over the place.

You may wish to have a Strategic Change Event, a kick-off to this new way of life. Everybody in the facility should be invited – *all* staff, families, community members, regulators, local legislators and the press. Say it out loud, say it publicly: "From this moment on we are all about home."

BUMP'S LAW
- What does the resident want?
- How did the resident do it at home?
- How do you do it at home?
- How should we do it here?

Learning Company Strategy:

The Steering Team works to create a sustainable and highly adaptive organization that is continually and consciously learning and transforming itself to be the desired context for its consumers. Besides changing it into a resident-centered (and ultimately, resident-*directed*) organization, you are changing it into a *changing* facility.

Resident care in the Household Model not only may be given differently than in a traditional facility, it also changes from resident to resident and from day to day. Look at how we do breakfast, for example.

We offer residents choices in what and when they eat. The choices Mrs. Roberts makes are different than Mr. Johnson's. And, Mrs. Roberts may like orange juice and a muffin every morning at 6:30 a.m. But, one day she may decide she doesn't like orange juice anymore and wants to sleep until 8.

To be resident directed, we must accommodate the human propensity to change one's mind. You are not changing from "A" to "B," you are changing from "A" to whatever darn letter the residents choose.

Growing into the new way of being begins *now*. Since most of the learning is done on the job much of it will be about adjusting to change – the new way-things-are-done. Instead of using a med cart, you may design how to keep medication in residents' rooms. Whoever dispenses meds will have to learn a new way. Everyone will experience this to some degree.

Learning a new and preferred way requires a seamless, fluid flow of information. Staff should be open to feedback from other workers, residents and families. There should be lots and lots of easily accessible opportunities for that information to come back to those involved throughout the organization. Mostly, this means communication should be open and honest so feedback is constant – not just in satisfaction surveys. Naturally, feedback also should be solicited by asking questions. Adjustments are made as needed, not only during times of formal training. Within this process, critical thinking abounds and everyone is empowered to interplay with open flow.

Profound change necessitates and stimulates learning at every level of individual and group awareness. Individuals must shift their thinking from unconscious, instant analysis of issues to thoughtful, collaborative inquiry that challenges long-held assumptions. We must acquire new abilities in tasks outside our usual job responsibilities; become more knowledgeable in the art of group dynamics, organizational development and adult learning; develop new skills in critical thinking and ways to motivate and engage people; and forever grow our individual humanity and organizational sense of self. There is more on learning in the chapter on organizational transformation.

"To be resident directed, we must accommodate the human propensity to change one's mind. You are not changing from "A" to "B," you are changing from "A" to whatever darn letter the residents choose."

"Individuals must shift their thinking from unconscious, instant analysis of issues to thoughtful, collaborative inquiry that challenges long-held assumptions."

Community Building With Elders Strategy:

As a society we are beginning to question the lack of autonomy and good quality of life for elders in long-term care. In the meantime, we providers must lead in shaping a responsive, small home that encourages frail elders to take charge to the degree they would if living in their previous home with all the support needed for a fulfilling life.

Discuss with elders the various community components that need to be brought together to accomplish this. Create opportunities for elders to solve their own problems the way other adults do. Help residents become acquainted with each other.

While waiting for a learning circle to begin, I overheard two female residents talking together. It turned out they had lived next to each other for six months and had never met. They decided it was time to meet regularly to chat, the way neighbors do.

Residents at Wesley Retirement Home in Des Moines, Iowa, told staff one thing they wanted out of the physical renovation of their home was a place to host – a place to have dinner and visit with family and friends, a place where they could offer a drink or some cookies, a place where they could share their home.

To build community, you must foster links to the outside world to give residents opportunities to give of themselves. Maybe you have a resident who until she entered the facility was giving piano lessons. See if you can arrange for students to continue their lessons at the facility. Partner with local charities elders can join as volunteers. There are as many possibilities as there are people in your community.

LEADERSHIP
Introduce
The Quest Begins
We Must...But How
We Commit & Resolve
We Align

WE ALIGN

You have planned and packed for your journey. It is time to recap your efforts and go over your checklist. You have aligned the assets and resources of the organization around the development of the Household Model. You know what and how much is available in time, talent, skills and dollars.

One and all are aligned as a team. Self-led teams are the norm for study, planning, design and development. Existing operational units (departments, hall areas, etc.) have begun using teams to make real decisions. Halls where residents live have been subdivided into workable "neighborhoods" of less than 25 people. Each neighborhood has permanently assigned staff from nursing, dietary, activities and housekeeping. All other employees are assigned adjunct roles.

All staff is 100 percent engaged in learning to work as a team and in participating in team-skills training. Team members are conducting some aspects of training, like in-services to prepare for households and PersonFirst™ techniques. (See *Living and Working in Harmony*.) Each

"We providers must lead in shaping a responsive, small home that encourages frail elders to take charge to the degree they would if living in their previous home with all the support needed for a fulfilling life."

staff person works on a hall, neighborhood or Action Team that focuses on a specific element of organizational life related to a specific group of residents. Everyone participates as part of a team in self-assessment and monitoring.

For every individual, personal values are coming to life. Little miracles are happening everywhere. Relationships are forming and personal stories are being shared. You are ready to redesign the organizational systems, environment and structure.

chapter 9
Organizational Transformation

contributing co-author: Linda Bump

"A community needs a soul if it is to become a true home for human beings. You, the people, must give it this soul."
- Pope John Paul II

ORGANIZATIONAL

Provoke the System

Embrace Chaos

We Develop

We Implement Change

Org. Becomes Ever Learning

WE PROVOKE THE SYSTEM

As you come together to commit to the course of the Household Model, you recognize that the organization must change in deep and sustainable ways. The real host of the illness that has debilitated long-term care is the organization. Not the individuals in the organization, but the culture and structure of the organization and all the external systems that surround it (regulations, associations, vendors, etc). Based on the belief that people are merely passing through (as if in a hospital) and focused on the medical care (as if in a hospital), the organization was structured efficiently for these purposes. This results in a one-size-fits all model of care that fosters top-down direction, task-oriented performance and institutional atmosphere.

Proof? There are 16,000 plus nursing homes in the country and all (except for Household and Green House models) are structured in *exactly* the same way! Anyone could recite the departments and positions in any nursing home in any town in any state. Top down, the tasks and responsibilities are broken up into job descriptions so narrow and specific that staff members often say, "It's not my job." While current leadership and staff are most assuredly not to blame for the existence or failures of these current operating systems, they are the keys to reforming the organization.

So, you must take a good look at the structure of the organization and, at the same time, not focus negatively on people and the resistance they provide. You have seen the things that are not "home" and do not honor the elders, such as getting folks up two hours before breakfast and parking them outside the dining room to wait. You know that is a practice that must change and perhaps you've already changed it in your early culture change efforts. To change it, the organizational structures that put the waking schedule into practice must be changed.

In the early stages of organizational transformation it is important that teams talk out loud about what works and what doesn't. The new, shared vision will have changed your standards and the emerging leadership that we identified in the previous chapter will reveal knowledge that was hidden until now.

Sharing information within and among teams should be in the form of dialogue rather than discussion or debate. Dialogue happens when everyone puts in his or her piece to make the full picture. You're not trying to figure out the best vantage point from which to look, you are taking in all views to understand the most complete view. It is more about contributing than persuading. We do it all the time in our own lives at

"The real host of the illness that has debilitated long-term care is the organization. Not the individuals in the organization, but the culture and structure of the organization..."

"You're not trying to figure out the best vantage point from which to look, you are taking in all views to understand the most complete view."

home. Our family weighs in with their schedules when trying to figure out a transportation plan or what and when to eat together – a lot of the same issues that we face in our organizations. Using dialogue as the mode of communication models household behavior. Through this process, the team begins to value working together above individual performance, and the concept of "team" really starts to take hold.

With dialogue, the team moves into a strategic thinking process to review the organizational structure and revamp the-way-we-do-things. This is not about the decision to put wallpaper borders in the bathroom to make it more inviting. Rather, it is about the process by which you come to those kinds of decisions. The power of implementing learning circles in your organization to change the way you communicate was discussed in an earlier chapter. Similarly, merely implementing a meeting model based on shared leadership with its new and efficient meeting practices will begin to change the way you do things. (See *Living and Working in Harmony*) Meetings are necessary – vital to the conduct of any business. Their importance as an imposed device of interpersonal communication increases as the size of an organization increases. Leaders often recognize this need and increase the number, frequency and length of meetings. They are then frustrated because they do not see fruitful results. In fact, there is often backlash among the staff (and managers alike). Everybody begins to feel they are "meetinged to death" and the only answer is to eliminate meetings in order to be productive.

Read about difference between dialogue and discussion: **www. thedialoguegrouponline. com/whatsdialogue. html#Contrast**

To put meetings back on track, leaders must:

- Understand the value and purpose of meetings to the household

- Structure meetings to carry out the functions indicated in this value and purpose

- Relegate activities that are unrelated to the value and purpose but have found their way into meetings to other methods of communication or activities.

There are two meeting structures that can make better use of your time and get more accomplished during a meeting: the team meeting model and the stand-up meeting.

The Team Meeting Model

To help the team get through a meeting most effectively, team members volunteer to fulfill the following roles during a meeting (from the workbook *Champions for Change* by LaVrene Norton). Be sure to take turns with each role so that everyone has a chance to strengthen different skills.

Team Meeting Roles

Meeting Leader: Focus the team on outcomes, work with the team to determine the agenda, to determine the time needed and the process to be used, and then lead the team to follow the agenda. When necessary, make decisions to move the process toward the stated outcomes.

Coach: Observe the process, advise the meeting leader and reflect observations on the process back to the entire team. Assure that everyone has an opportunity to share. Gently intervene to reduce excessive talking, to bring people back on track and to acknowledge agreement and conflict.

Timekeeper: Have a clear understanding from the leader or team as to time ("How much time do we want to spend on this activity?") And then periodically remind the team as time winds down. ("We have seven minutes left, we have two minutes left," etc.) Point out excessive deviation from agenda ("We had planned to spend 15 minutes on the item, it's now 20 – do we continue, and for how long and what do we drop off our agenda to compensate for it?")

Scribe: Record on the flip chart or take notes as per meeting or meeting leader's direction. Should work to record words as stated, without rewording. Record attendance, key content of discussion, actions steps and outcomes. Distribute copies of notes to all attendees.

Welcomer (optional but highly recommended to strengthen involvement in the team): Starts off meeting with a bit of inspiration; good news, interesting and relevant article, poem, etc. May also be in charge of refreshments when appropriate. Residents often love this role as they can prepare for it ahead of time and know that they are making a serious contribution.

 You can see how putting team members in these roles will keep things running smoothly.

Stand-up Meeting

While the model above works best for longer meetings where multiple topics are addressed, the stand-up meeting is a great way to tackle specific issues that need to be addressed outside of scheduled meeting times.

The stand-up meeting, or huddle, is just that - a meeting where everyone who attends, stands up, usually in a small circle or huddle. Psychologically and physically it reminds the group that the meeting will be quick and therefore everyone should stay focused and on target.

The process of communication is through rounds, similar to the learning circle. Participants take turns sharing their thoughts. Immediate and spontaneous feedback to the individual sharing is not allowed. However, depending upon your purpose, rules can be developed to either allow or prohibit a second round for questions and feedback. Other rules for individual and group behavior can be established to reinforce your purpose and process.

The stand-up meeting is an excellent means of frequent and regular communication within a self-led team. It is of great value when a number of individuals in different roles share in resident care. It improves the flow of communication; allows frequent understandings of each other's roles, concerns and frustrations; and guarantees frequent opportunities to vent feelings. The stand-up meeting can improve team spirit and resolve daily operational problems – both major contributors to increased productivity and employee satisfaction. The stand-up meeting has a specific purpose, a clear process or agenda and a specified length, which must be faithfully adhered to.

 Leader's steps in facilitating a stand-up meeting:

1. Determine the purpose for the meeting. It may be one or more of the following: increase team spirit; share feedback to one another; share knowledge and information about operations, policy changes or residents with each other; give updates on household or organization-wide changes; vent daily frustrations; share one's daily work plans with others to determine overlaps, gaps, etc.; update as the day goes on and a staff member or two goes home and others come in to work; or any other topic that needs to be addressed.

2. Consider the number of staff to be involved and what it is you want them to share. Then, determine the length of the meeting. For example, you have four staff starting the morning in the household that you want to involve. Your primary purpose is to increase team spirit. You wish to have them accomplish this by setting the right mood for their work and sharing their daily work

plans to determine how they can help each other. You decide to meet for a maximum of 5 minutes in a stand-up after the fourth person arrives (you have staggered work times but all four are in the house by 9:30 and breakfast is usually winding down. You've found that just stopping and standing in the kitchen for five minutes to go over the day works great. You always decide at that time who will facilitate the morning learning circle with residents and staff – that usually takes place about 10:30 a.m.

3. As leader, spend no more than one minute in introduction – setting the mood, motivating or outlining the topic for the meeting

4. Have each person share his or her feelings or concerns about the day's work or the topic at hand.

5. Let it be your responsibility to make note (mental or actual) of all comments so that you may summarize and respond to any questions left unanswered.

6. End on a motivational, upbeat note. "Let's make it a great day!" or….

The stand-up meeting is also a great way to get out quick news to everyone at the same time. Often, when something comes up a future formal meeting is planned. By meeting time, the news has made its way through the grapevine, everybody has a slightly different view of the news and the meeting seems useless because the word is out already or more time is given to the meeting than needed. The stand up meeting serves as a healthy alternative. Consider keeping a notebook in a kitchen drawer for recording the date, time and summary of the meeting. Now anyone can catch up if they've missed a day.

"The stand-up meeting is also a great way to get out quick news to everyone at the same time."

"For deep change to occur, you must go through painful unlearning of the things that created the structure you wish to change."

"We commonly think residents become institutionalized and cling to routine, but so do staff."

Deep Change Requires Painful Unlearning

For deep change to occur, you must go through painful unlearning of the things that created the structure you wish to change. It is "painful" because each of you will have to look honestly at how you personally have supported a system that does not adequately or justly serve the elders to whom you're committed. This means being self-aware and thinking deeply about your actions so as not to fall into the old habits you've decided to leave behind. We commonly think residents become institutionalized and cling to routine, but so do staff. The team must break down the current system and build a new one. Not only will the new model be different, the means of building it will be different as well. For help with the painful unlearning of institutionalism, refer to Norton's Ten Challenges of deep culture change (from *Ever Learning – a Workbook for Organizational Change*).

 Ask team members to think about how they will overcome the following challenges:

1. Divisions and barriers resulting from departmental silos, wide variety of tasks and multiple shifts caring for the same individuals with minimal opportunity to communicate and plan or coordinate how to best meet resident needs.

2. Dramatic differences in experience, education and pay between direct service and management staff.

3. Traditional hierarchy grown historically out of the hospital model (originally from the military) and sustained and encouraged through regulatory actions and organizational fear about compliance and financial viability.

4. Societal attitudes toward elders and their inclusion and value.

5. Elders as inadequately informed and unengaged consumers.

6. Opportunities for critical thinking limited to those in management, with positions close to the resident reduced to performing tasks defined and detailed by others.

7. Leadership limited by extensive management and minimal leadership experience.

8. Societal attitude toward nursing homes that demoralizes staff and residents, and lowers expectations and heightens demands by family members.

9. Inability to envision alternatives to institutional care for large numbers of elders.

10. Limited resources tightly administered through a regulated infrastructure without genuine oversight by the direct consumer.

You may think we are being dramatic by using the phrase "painful unlearning." But while each challenge presented above may in and of itself be painfully difficult to overcome, the more significant unlearning is to first overcoming the thinking that only "managers" can talk about these things. The team of formal and informal leaders as well as future households with residents and families can openly discuss these issues and, as a result, grow in their commitment to the vision.

The Learning Company

We've looked to Peter Senge and *The Fifth Discipline* to learn about systems and creating a "learning company." Systems like those in a long-term care organization are bound by interrelated actions. All parts are necessary and should be seen together as a whole, not individually. Change in one area affects all others. So all areas must be addressed in order to bring about profound change.

Determining what's for breakfast and how and where it is eaten, for example, requires support from all over the organization and across multiple shifts. The services of dietary, nursing and clinical care, housekeeping, laundry, pharmacy, maintenance; therapy and the timing of doctors' visits; accounting and purchasing; regulations; the layout of the facility and, of course, the elders' desires are all simultaneously in play. It is more like building a house of cards than knocking down a trail of dominos. Interrelationships in balance as opposed to chains of cause and effect make up the structure. This is not just a new way of looking at things. This *is* how things are. Only now do you see it clearly. What has changed is the way you act around and within the system. You create the future instead of reacting to the present. The-way-things-are today will never change until you start looking at the way things could and should be tomorrow – until you are thinking not one step ahead but in a new dimension. It is the difference between *letting* things happen *to* you, and *making* things happen *for* you in your shared vision of resident directed service.

You must leave behind the way things were and start fresh – everyone at point A. Think of a theater company. Its goal is to put on a play and the actors are assembled for that purpose. They approach the situation with open minds because the scenic director can't plan the scenery without knowing the size of the actors, where they move, what their costumes may be and the layout of the stage. The actors cannot know exactly how they will perform a scene until they know where the props are on stage, what parts of the stage are lit and when, and what time the play will be performed. All people involved move together as a team – supporting each other, each adding their essential element. Lights, sound, music, acting, scene, costumes, tickets, venue, publicity – all are equally important and nothing is put in place without the other components. You will create home in the same manner, but with the elders as directors.

Patching up the existing organization will not do. If you put the dietary department to work redesigning breakfast, you will have a new way of doing breakfast but it may prove to be unworkable for Certified Nurse Assistants (CNAs). Then, perhaps, the CNAs make adjustments that

"It is more like building a house of cards than knocking down a trail of dominos. Interrelationships in balance as opposed to chains of cause and effect make up the structure."

"You create the future instead of reacting to the present."

"Patching up the existing organization will not do."

throw off the administration of medications. The entire plan deteriorates rapidly. And more likely, the idea doesn't make it to the planning stage much less become implemented because everyone, assuming failure, is resisting the change. So, when changes are made, they must be made in a high involvement fashion. All of the cards in the deck must be involved in the shuffle.

Those desiring a change must understand the need to take time to do it right by addressing the system as a whole and building from the ground up. You may be tempted to trade systemic change for instant gratification, but that will only hurt in the long run. A friend once said of raising children, "You either do the work early when they are little or you end up doing more work when they are older." The *Cliff Notes* or *Culture Change for Dummies* will not work. Full understanding is broad and deep. It is achieved when everybody knows all the angles and the whole system learns at the same time. Knowledge and power are not for an elite few. Knowledge and power must be distributed widely and solidly placed in the hands of the elders, their families and the caregivers.

In the last episode of The Mary Tyler Moore Show the whole gang is in a group hug in the middle of the office. Some are crying and we hear a voice from the middle of the huddle say "I need a tissue." The group, still hugging, shuffles in the direction of a desk upon which rests a box of tissue. The person closest to the tissue grabs one and passes it to the one in need. That is systemic functioning. A situation arises and together, everyone responds.

For an organization to really flourish, it must be a "learning organization." In this sense, "learning" is not just taking in information that is then "known." Learning is a state of being. Ambivalence, or even being reactive is not enough for a learning organization.

Senge says in *The Fifth Discipline*, "...the basic meaning of a 'learning organization' (is) an organization that is continually expanding its capacity to create its future."

As systems adapt or are redesigned to be strongly in sync with the organization's values, yours will also become a learning company.

No, we were not kidding about the "deep" part of deep change. As you now face the organizational change phase you may once again feel overwhelmed. But, the good news is, as Senge says, "We are all learners." We have practiced growing and improving all our lives. The increasing body of knowledge about change, systems and learning merge with increasingly strong team skills to prepare you for this next step.

"Those desiring a change must understand the need to take time to do it right by addressing the system as a whole and building from the ground up."

Ways to Provoke the System

You began provoking the system when you formed the Steering Team You see things differently. You continuously ask questions of each other. You seek knowledge. You learned new ways to actually be a team. You work within the Steering Team and the Action Teams you formed. You've made many changes as you are mapping out your household future.

And as long-term care folks always are, you're ready to do something. It may be another year or even two before you move into households, so what must you do now?

As explained in the Leadership chapter, be aggressive about involvement. Get everyone – 100 percent of staff and residents and as many families as possible – involved. Create genuine dialogue everywhere.

In his book *Business Systems Engineering,* Gregory H. Watson said, "Strategy is the persistence of a vision. It is the art of seeing differently, and then planning to act differently. It is the combined ability of a group to see where it wants to go, to see where it is, and to identify what must be done to close this gap, and then to execute those changes that are necessary to get and stay on track that will close this gap. For a vision to persist, it must be carried out over time. Persistent visions are therefore aligned with the long-term business objectives that state what must be done to close the gap."

We recommend using these strategies to get your *whole* organization involved:

1. Strategic Planning Process: Strategic planning is a formal means of bringing the entire community into the Household Model's revolutionary change process while helping ensure what is created has broad support and commitment. Equally important, strategic planning produces a values-driven roadmap for all stakeholders to use in closing the gap between the organization's existing institutional structure and the Household Model.

There are a variety of approaches to strategic planning. Of course, you need to design or select that which works best with your organizational dynamics and culture. In building a new culture, it is all the more important to put considerable thought into strategic planning.

Many consultants facilitate multiple sessions over a period of several months. It can be difficult to keep large numbers of people engaged over such a long period of time. We recommend the "Five-Day Submersion" approach to strategic planning. This approach is designed to firmly ground the organization in its values and strategies in a short timeframe.

"Create genuine dialogue everywhere."

The process starts Monday morning and ends Friday morning with a completed plan bound and ready to review for approval. On Monday, all the invited stakeholders gather. Tuesday through Thursday are filled with specific breakout planning sessions. On Friday morning all stakeholders reconvene to review the plan, make adjustments and approve it to be considered for formal adoption.

The process involves the following framework guidelines:

Engage a Facilitator - Unless you have a seasoned facilitator on staff, contracting with an outside consultant may be the most effective way to bring your stakeholders together and provide a framework for strategic planning. Even if you do have such a person on staff, it still may be better to bring in someone with no previous involvement with the organizational dynamics. Strategic planning, done well, is one of the most important tools for assuring the organization's survival and growth. It's not a time for skimping…you generally get what you pay for. Perhaps you have little or no experience assembling a wide collection of organizational stakeholders together at one time. Ensuring the facilitator is seasoned to group process will help maximize the impact of your investment.

Invite Everybody and Their Dog - Several weeks before the event, send formal invitations to residents, families, staff and board members, corporate officers, vendors, community leaders, elected officials, surveyor agencies, the ombudsman, volunteers--everybody you can think of who has a stake in the organization. Describe the five-day process and invite them to help shape their own futures by helping shape the organization. You may be surprised at the response.

Form a Week Long Planning Support Team - Completing a strategic plan in one workweek takes teamwork. Organizing feedback into an articulate document requires a designated support team operating behind the scenes throughout the week. The *facilitator* is the team leader and all other team members should rally around his or her leadership.

The facilitator should capture each general and breakout session as it occurs on flip charts or other media viewable by participants. In addition, a *scribe* with a laptop must be in each session to transcribe everything that is said for reference (along with the facilitator's flipchart documentation) at the end of each day throughout the week.

The *designated support team* should organize the notes from each session into a draft to be inserted into the final document. The assigned teams complete their work each day so the strategic plan is crafted in tandem with how the process progresses throughout the week. This requires working in the evenings so each day's notes are completed before sessions begin the next day.

Planning Sessions

Monday – Made up of general sessions involving all invited stakeholders. The sessions below are designed to give participants a global view of the organization and the environment in which it operates. Mission, vision and values also are covered on the first day to ensure as many people as possible participate in forming the organization's identity.

Morning Sessions

Welcome and Introductions – The participants are welcomed, introductions are made and the overall weeklong planning process is described. All participants are invited to stay the full day, and to sign up for the Tuesday-Thursday breakout sessions and the Friday morning closing session where they will be asked to review and approve the final plan draft.

Organizational History - The first part of the morning can be spent reviewing the organization's history and what has led to the present day. This can also include a review and update of the most recent strategic plan.

Long-Term Care Trends – The facilitator should provide a "Thirty Thousand Foot" view of the long-term care sector including present and future trends. This gives all the stakeholders a solid context of the universe in which the organization gravitates.

Mission and Vision – The facilitator guides the group in evaluating the existing mission and vision statements respectively and determining if changes are desired. These should be short, well thought out statements that fit on stationary headings, business cards or other collateral documents. The mission statement should clearly state the organization's purpose. The vision statement should, in the form of a tag line, capture the organization's essence by describing its character, how it lives out its mission and its impact.

Afternoon Session

Values - The facilitator should make this a free-flow process by inviting everyone in the room (which is usually full) to share words, phrases or sentences reflecting what is important to them about the organization's beliefs, and what is held dear. Words will begin to fly about the room to be captured by the facilitator and scribe. The facilitator should ask the group's permission to have their thoughts summarized and organized on paper for the group to review during the Friday morning general session. The opportunity for review will prevent "wordsmithing" by those actively participating while maximizing the group's creativity. Though participants usually agree to have their ideas recorded, it is important to seek their permission. In the evening, the support team and/or the facilitator will organize all the words, phrases, and sentences in a way that best represents the collective will and vision expressed by the group.

Tuesday Through Thursday - Breakout sessions are scheduled for a suggested duration of one and a half hours per topic. Sign up sheets for these sessions are offered in the general session. Organizers should ensure there is a good, solid cross section of stakeholders in each session by recruiting additional members if the signup sheets don't sufficiently represent the organizational make-up.

The facilitator should encourage sessions to be conducted in a circle. Circles are powerful and equalizing. The facilitator should remind the group that everybody is equal and encourage full participation.

Breakout session topics should be identified in advance of the strategic planning process. These topics should reflect the categories that need strategic focus in the year(s) ahead. You may also wish to include an "other" category to ensure all ideas not considered in specific breakout sessions are presented.

The following are a few of the many issues that could or should be included as breakout session topics:

> Plant and Asset Management
>
> Services (i.e. Nursing, Dining, etc.)
>
> Lifestyle and Service Character
>
> People, Organizational Structure and Culture
>
> Board/Ownership Development
>
> Learning and Teaching
>
> Marketing
>
> Finance
>
> Information Technology
>
> Grounds
>
> Strategic Relationships
>
> Organizational Positioning

Friday Morning Closing Session - The facilitator, scribe and support team(s) have had a long week of assembling information that reflects the sessions, so on Friday morning they are generally tired yet proud of the comprehensive document they have created. By Thursday night, most support teams are genuinely amazed at the plan's comprehensiveness. Some groups bookend their documents with introductory and closing letters by organizational leaders (i.e. Community Mentor, Board Chair, Owner, Social Worker, Household Team Member).

The facilitator presents the plan to the reassembled group via power point or overhead projector. Often there are clarifications, further discussion about certain points and suggested changes. Once these are done, the broad group of participants are usually "proud as punch" of their impressive document that truly reflects the organization. The facilitator asks for a vote or other form of approval to forward the plan to the ownership or board of directors for adoption. Some groups have participants sign a page that symbolically reflects individual and group endorsement. Some even have pictures taken of the entire group with somebody holding the plan in front.

If the plan truly reflects the week's happenings, significant strides are made in five short days in aligning the whole organization around its purpose and beliefs.

2. Strategic Change Event: The strategic change event is another group process for introducing change to all – staff, residents, families, but also community leaders, politicians, media, ombudsmen and Board members. It can precede strategic planning or serve more as a final step in the move to households. The Strategic Change Event is structured to encourage everyone in the organization and its surrounding community to "turn on a dime" – dramatically shifting the energy from being resigned to the institutional way to eagerly moving in sync toward the Household Model. People come together for three to four days to explore the changes that have already taken place and participate in the planning for those that are yet to come. Sessions are held on all areas of household life – dietary to activities, self-led teams to elder counsel. The different sessions run all day long and attendees are invited to take part in as many sessions as they like. When Action Pact facilitates strategic change events, they make sure the agendas for each day are published and posted throughout the facility as well in local newspapers and community bulletin boards. People will talk about how life in households will be different. It is both a symbolic and literal turning point for all involved.

These events are usually most effective with an outside consultant facilitating the process. (see Workbook – *Creating Home – a Strategic Change Event* by LaVrene Norton)

Wesley Retirement Services of Des Moines, IA held strategic change events at all five of their retirement communities as a means of engaging all stakeholders. Each Wesley retirement community is in a different Iowa city and had unique environments and individualized culture change plans. All were moving as close to households as possible, some with low cost renovations and others with extensive renovation and new construction.

At the Village in Indianola, IA the architects were present as residents shared what they needed in order to feel truly at home. The new households had to have personal and community spaces as well as continuous access to hosting foods in order to continue their life-long pleasures of inviting family and friends into their homes. The architects went back to the drawing board and modified their plans.

At Park Center in Newton, IA, a couple of nurses, still a little resistant, shared a table with family members and a resident. Before their session was over they had together visualized a home where they each could continue the good life they currently led. They left open to possibilities.

3. Organizational Design Action Teams: The Steering Team can begin to create daily excitement in the organization and get to the hard work of re-organization done at the same time by forming Action Teams. These teams, with staff from various function areas, begin by studying other transforming organizations, especially those moving toward or operating in households. The teams begin to plan for decentralization of all traditional operating systems. Dining, med pass, care-planning, MDS and activities become household centered. The Steering Team and its Action Teams must think through every system. How will the household plan menus? Prepare meals? Serve meals? Get people to their household dining room? What about snacks? When will meals be served? How will therapies be done? How will social services meet the needs of the residents? How will activities work? Will everyone do activities? Teams and the organization as a whole will figure out how to put their values into action in the future households. They will determine how households will work with areas that remain centralized such as human resources, purchasing, business office and reception. Finally, they will decide the parameters of the household teams. They will determine how different the teams can be

ORGANIZATIONAL

Provoke the System

Embrace Chaos

We Develop

We Implement Change

Org. Becomes Ever Learning

from one household to another.

 Form Action Teams to begin focusing on the options (and opportunities) for your organizational transformation in:

Structure and Accountabilities – address the overall structure of the organization.

Human Resources – address job descriptions and blended roles

Nursing Services – address liberalizing of diets and meds (hopefully much of it has already been accomplished in early culture change efforts); med pass, staffing and scheduling.

Dining Services – address the options for making the kitchen the heart of your households - hopefully to deepen the change that has already been made in your earlier work to change the culture of dining in your organization. (See the Action Pact workbook, *Making the Kitchen the Heart of the Home* for ideas on the transformation of dining at every stage along your journey to households.)

WE EMBRACE EMERGING CHAOS

As you begin to tear down and rebuild, things may seem a little chaotic, in fact, sometimes more than a little. You may have the urge to "put things back." Those staff members who are less certain and lack vision will surely have that urge. Instead, think again of the vision – bringing authority and decisions as close to the elders as possible. Bring some order to the chaos by focusing energy on designing for decentralization.

Introducing Self-led Teams

Begin to plan for decentralization of authority by developing the self-led teams that will make up the organization. During this period of transition, most leadership staff (and hopefully most other staff due to your commitment to high involvement) will be working simultaneously in the present and the future, maintaining the current traditional operational systems to assure the delivery of quality care and regulatory compliance while designing the new systems that will support the vision of deep

"Begin to plan for decentralization of authority by developing the self-led teams that will make up the organization."

culture change in your emerging households.

It is critical to maintain your current systems that have served you and your residents well in the past until your new systems are clearly formalized to assure continuity in care and compliance during the actual transition. You've already practiced this through the Steering Team and Action Team process.

While your households are still under construction, begin the shift of department head responsibilities to the self-led teams of the future households. You will have chosen your household leadership by now. Ask, "What are our responsibilities?" and, "How can we get that responsibility into the household, as close to the elder as possible?" Look at all department leadership, manager and supervisor job descriptions. What functions and tasks must be included into the household team's accountabilities? What tasks must be retained by licensed professionals, both clinical and other professionals?

As your action teams work to define future responsibilities and training needs for the self-led teams, start with considering the essentials for maintaining quality of care and service with regulatory compliance. Remember that it is positive outcomes we are seeking, and that the way we achieve these outcomes is limited only by our creativity and willingness to embrace change. Always ask, "Why not?" whenever confronted with an obstacle to change. Keeping the goal in sight, and continually questioning any tendency to maintain the status quo, will lead your teams to new heights of self-direction and quality outcomes.

At one organization, staff came together in planning groups with their current job descriptions in hand. They came prepared to literally cut up their job descriptions. They placed the pieces with the functions that they felt they must continue to be responsible for in the new household structure on the table close to them. Others they placed into the center of the table. These were functions that could be re-configured or re-grouped into new jobs to be carried out by others in the households.

This is the time when teams brainstorm, consider, discuss and eventually learn their new responsibilities and then ultimately plan for and undergo training. Teams should review various training tools in the *Household Matters* kit especially the in-service and orientation training ideas in the *Living and Working in Harmony* section. Additional training materials are available from Action Pact on www.culturechangenow.com.

"Remember that it is positive outcomes we are seeking, and that the way we achieve these outcomes is limited only by our creativity and willingness to embrace change."

This is the time to begin planning for the time when all staff members receive their permanent assignments to households. This includes not only the care-giving staff, but all those moving from dietary, housekeeping, social services, activities and department head functions. This is the time to begin planning for when nurses are assigned and retrained as needed to assume other roles that may have been centralized under the previous operating system. These employees will, at move-in, be accountable through a household instead of reporting through a department.

So, now you are in the thick of it. Even though your organization has been talking and planning for awhile, when you start to lay out the-way-things-will-be people may finally say, "Oh my gosh! This is really happening!" It may be that now, and not until this moment, do you think, "My job - my life will change!" But it's merely a moment of panic - that moment when you're ready to forever commit yourself to a new life. Similar to the moments before the birth of the baby, these are merely jitters. You've already carefully thought things through, detailed all the contingencies, bought the larger house and are now getting closer to moving in. We bring the baby home before we fully understand all the implications of a life changed by parenthood.

Similarly, organizations are often deeply committed and well along the culture change journey before they genuinely understand all the implications of the transformation they've undertaken. They have heard it discussed and seen evidence of it in places they visit but still do not fully realize all its aspects, much less its impact on each and every person involved in the organization. The idea of all residents and staff being involved in the decisions of daily life sounds right but almost impossible to fully understand until you begin to experience it in practice. However, each organization on the household path suddenly comes to realize they are talking about eliminating departments, repositioning formal leaders who will often pitch in to help in their households and strengthening direct-service positions with leadership responsibilities. The process can be frightening as chaos ramps up throughout the organization. Even well-intended formal leaders who felt ready for change and participated in setting the timetable can become frightened in these last minutes before move-in.

"The idea of all residents and staff being involved in the decisions of daily life sounds right but almost impossible to fully understand until you begin to experience it in practice."

Robert E. Quinn describes the scene well in his book, *Change the World: How Ordinary People Can Accomplish Extraordinary Results*. "New realities emerge, demanding new responses. At this point people and groups within the hierarchy may become threatened and self-serving in renewed resistance, insisting that their way of operating in the organization works...They lose touch with emergent reality, choosing instead to live in the past, where their vision and knowledge worked."

Surprises are in store as individuals who everyone thought would be fine are discombobulated and individuals who everyone predicted would leave the organization are happy as clams.

The Household Model was conceptually embraced by the LPNs at one transforming organization until this stage of the journey when they realized that the way they had successfully cared for the elders for the past 20+ years was, in fact, going to change. I was presenting at a state conference more than a year after the LPNs' facility had transformed into households. There were a couple hundred folks in the audience, including one of the LPNs. We opened for questions at the end and the LPN took the mike from the roving facilitator and asked me if she could come onto the stage. I knew she thought the residents were happier in the households – she had told me that on my last visit to her facility – but I also knew she and her colleagues had strongly opposed eliminating med carts. I was still a little anxious. She came up and told the audience, "I opposed this change with every energy. I just did not think we could get the right meds to the right people at the right time without med carts. Now that we do this every day, I cannot imagine it any other way and I would never go back. They have a good life everyday in the households. I used to leave work every day grieving for the things I could not do for my residents, now I leave every day, dead tired, but thinking of the many good things I was able to do for them today and plan to do for them tomorrow. "

Teams need strong resolve to weather this difficult time and leadership must hold to the vision and never waver. Their shared vision will ultimately unite them in deep satisfaction.

This is the time to design for the future. Action Teams should make recommendations to the Steering Team for consideration. In the next stage you develop the specific system designs, policies and procedures to support the visioning and planning completed in the current stage, but for now, begin to consider your recommendations for:

- Organization chart and job descriptions – Recommend the options that best match your organization's human resources.
- Training – This includes training for all staff on communication and team skills and competencies. (See *Living and Working in Harmony*) It is time for everyone to begin to learn the new way-

"Surprises are in store as individuals who everyone thought would be fine are discombobulated and individuals who everyone predicted would leave the organization are happy as clams."

things-are-done.

- Cross-training – Plan to offer cross-training to everyone. The more versatile workers you have the better. This training includes formal CNA training as well as dietary and activities training. Incentives should be offered to those willing to cross-train.

- Posting of household jobs – Decide the process for selection, and begin to form the communication method.

- Assignment to households – Decide the process for making permanent assignments to households. While the actual assignments should be made and instituted a bit later, this is the time to plan for who will work where, who will work together, who will work with which residents. Plan now for some resistance to permanent assignments. It will come from staff who believe that they will burn out caring for certain residents. Others will fear getting too attached to residents, concerned that they will be unable to survive the deep reoccurring losses from the passing of so many close relationships.

- Team meetings of future household staff – Start planning for these meetings now. Perhaps you will choose to implement temporary households on wings or floors of your current facility prior to move-in to the new households, or perhaps you will wait for the real move day, but as soon as possible, start meeting as a household team and planning for your future as a household.

- Assignment of residents to households – Start planning now for the high involvement of residents and their families regarding where they will live in the new households. Prepare yourself for some resistance, remember that the fear of the unknown is as present for families and residents as for staff.

Mr. Edwards, as a resident in a traditional facility, had lost the motivation to engage fully in life. He had been active in his church, community and profession prior to being admitted to the nursing home for an acute medical decline immediately following the death of his wife. Now, he was committed to logging the inadequacy of the facility's response to his needs. When wheeled to the new construction site (while still in stud wall stage), he was able to select his own room. "This is the new nursing home?" he exclaimed. "If I have this room, I could put my desk right in front of the window and put a bird feeder in that tree. Life just might be good again!" Shortly after moving into the household, he set up

Bible study one evening a week. It was well attended by folks from his church and new friends from the households.

ORGANIZATIONAL

Provoke the System

Embrace Chaos

We Develop

We Implement Change

Org. Becomes Ever Learning

- Involvement of families, residents, staff in learning circles – Learning circles should become part of everyday life in households, and this is the time to commit to the practice. All team and household decisions should be addressed in this way. Also, learning circles on conversational topics will help staff and residents get to know each other and help set a tone for the household. Include family members whenever possible. And when the tendency to slip back into traditional memos and meetings occurs, remember that learning circles are key to relationship-based communication in a transforming organization.

- Move-in planning – It's not too early to begin participating in choices of interior design elements, furnishings, supplies, foods and items for gifting (We suggest registering at a department or discount store for housewarmings.) Once again, remember the importance of high involvement at every stage of the journey. While at this stage, these choices may be generic, or may just narrow the field of options for the future household team. Initial involvement by the action teams, and ultimately the household teams, will support the design of a true home for residents and staff.

WE DEVELOP AS CHAOS CLIMAXES

When organizations first talk of the Household Model, everyone's fears are about regulations. Earlier in the book we suggested that you needed to push through that fear, because it serves no purpose but to hold you back and to feed the resistance to change. But now you're ready to develop the systems that will replace the-way-things-are-done. Now is the time to carefully design a future that merges excellence in regulatory compliance with the pleasant daily life of home.

Maintaining Standards of Practice in System Design

The systems you design must be compliant with regulations. Everyone is so excited about moving into a household – residents are truly happy, laughter and hugs are spontaneous – that it is easy to forget those things that you *must* continue to do. You must continue to separate clean and dirty

"Now is the time to carefully design a future that merges excellence in regulatory compliance with the pleasant daily life of home."

dishes in the kitchen. You must wear a hair restraint when preparing food for a meal, even in the household kitchen. You must continue to schedule activities on a household calendar. You must support the resident's right to refuse a care or treatment through assessment, education on risk, and offering alternatives. While ensuring whatever and whenever a resident desires for breakfast becomes a new norm, you must be sure that all items on a posted menu for breakfast are available for service, even if *no* resident in your household *ever* chooses them. You must assure that care conferences are held within the Resident Assessment Instrument (RAI) timeline, even if a separate family meeting is held outside the timeline so more family members can attend. You must insist that a staff person sharing housekeeping and dining duties wear proper uniform for each task. You must realize that laundry soap is a potentially toxic substance and must be kept in a safe and locked place, even in the household laundry room. You must remember that proper hand washing is the first line of defense against food borne illness and offense in infection control.

Design and Development of the Systems Changes Required for Decentralization

We recognize that many systems, protocols and policies within the traditional nursing home model must be carried forth to the Household Model. The context for these systems, however, changes from institution to home, affecting the way we continue these necessary functions.

The following pages break down the service functions that are affected by the transition from the department structure to the Household Model. The accompanying *Creating Home* policies and procedures, *Living and Working in Harmony* integrated human resource system and *Reflection on Quality* process and measurement system are all designed within the Household Matters kit to support the organization in the areas outlined in the next section.

Designing and developing decentralized systems is both simple and complex. The values, principles and theories behind the changes in operating systems are simple – back to the basics of Chapter Four – your theory and vision put to practice guided by the Essential Elements. However, as you consider the interrelationships of systems and how they are implemented, the complexities arise. Here we will take a look at each system in more detail, driven by the Essential Elements for their design.

"We recognize that many systems, protocols and policies within the traditional nursing home model must be carried forth to the Household Model. The context for these systems, however, changes from institution to home, affecting the way we continue these necessary functions."

Dining

We often start with dietary because it allows for incremental shifts in resident service that often lead to highly visible and positive results and creates those "ah ha" moments that energize teams and the proocess of change. There are seemingly endless opportunities for change in Dietary, and each requires the development of a system to support it.

Life Around the Kitchen

There are big decisions that must be made around how food is prepared and served. Set a standard for the design work immediately. Move as close to living at home as possible. Many factors will hold you away from that ideal, but push through all that you can. Let's think of our own homes for a minute. Home life includes a kitchen that nurtures the family. We can find food there for a quick snack, an individualized meal or the makings of a family meal. We can find hydration there – that pleasant, cool glass of water, the milk and juices in the refrigerator, the fresh pot of coffee, the makings for tea. We find the table comfortable to sit at, reading the paper or a book, chatting with family or friend. We love to attend to family there. We wipe off the counter top, put the dishes in the dishwasher and go through recipe books thinking about dinner for friends on Saturday night. We have a grocery list that we keep on the fridge – anybody in the family can add to it. Preparing for this evening meal, we might make the dessert mid-morning or in the early afternoon. Someone sets the table early evening, while someone else finishes up the salad. As we sit down for the meal we pour our choice of water, milk, coffee. Bread and butter is put on the table and the salad served while we enjoy smells of the main course wafting their way from stove to table. Discussion of the day mixes delightfully with requests to pass the bread and butter.

Now step back – can you do it all? What major hurdles will have to be overcome?

Food Preparation

How and where will we prepare and deliver food? Consider cooking breakfast to order in the households. Households across the country start the day with this signature of culture change. To facilitate sleeping in and eating late, develop systems to serve your residents at the times they choose to eat, and be prepared to flex those systems as your residents come and go.

Remember too, it is not just the food preparation and service systems that must be redesigned, but also the nutritional assessment and care planning. Support this strong statement of resident preference against the institutional norm of regularly scheduled mealtimes with the documentation essential for regulatory compliance. How (and where) will lunch and supper be prepared and delivered? Will yours be one of the lucky nursing homes that has forward thinking fire marshalls and state regulators who will support the preparation of two, or even three meals a day in your household kitchens? When you consider the positive impact of breakfast to order on our residents' health and happiness, just imagine the impact of having all three meals to order. In the beginning consider cooking breakfast to order and preparing most desserts, salads and other special food items as part of household life. Keep your plans (both physical environment and operating systems) flexible to allow for future progression.

Staffing the Kitchen

There are three options you may consider for staffing the kitchen in the Household Model:

1. The creation of a homemaker position that incorporates dietary aide and housekeeping aide roles and responsibilities. This blend is logical and simple, generally playing to people's strengths. But don't think for a minute that all housekeepers love to cook, or all dietary folks love to clean. Just let the teams and the households work it out, and they will. Of course, continue to encourage all staff to become CNAs so they can better assist the residents in the dining experience.

2. The creation of versatile workers - all staff trained to perform tasks in dietary. If you choose this route, remember once again the rigors of regulatory compliance, especially when expecting all positions to have working knowledge of all kitchen functions.

3. Create a blend of dietary and activity aide hours into a kitchen activities position. This lucky person spends their whole day working with food and fun in the kitchen. Think about the time spent in your kitchen at home, and the range of tasks accomplished there, and you will sense the potential for this blend.

These are three of any number of blended roles you can design within a versatile household team to staff the kitchen.

Housekeeping

As explained above, housekeeping can be accomplished through blended homemaker roles. Housekeeping, however, is a responsibility of the entire household team. It's everybody's job. Each self-led team will self organize around expected standards and accountabilities.

Nursing

Yes, according to the services you offer and the regulations you honor, this *is* still a nursing home, and skilled at that. So we must also introduce the creation of home and the honoring of resident choice into the development of new nursing systems. Frequently the most difficult for staff to conceptualize, the development of these system changes will require the most skill in leading change in your organizational journey.

First, guided by the Essential Elements offered in Chapter Four, you develop new patterns for delivering nursing care, and reconsider the roles of all nursing staff. Develop systems to define the registered and licensed nurses' role in your households. Will they be full-time members of the household, assuming a great variety of roles in that household? Or, will they be neighborhood nurses, serving two or even three neighboring households in a less broad nursing role? In the formative stages of household model discovery, some organizations have chosen to have registered nurses act as visiting nurses entering the households only for defined nursing tasks at defined times of the day, just like home health services are delivered in our own communities today. We, the authors, do not recommend this approach. Remember the importance of keeping services close to the resident, and also of the myriad of opportunities for registered and licensed nurses to contribute their talents to the residents and the household team.

Key Nursing Systems Change

After you develop the systems for who does what in nursing, you need to develop the processes to honor individualized care in the delivery of nursing services. The hallmark systems changes in nursing revolve around the med pass and the MDS (Minimum Data Set) documentation process.

The options for individualizing med pass in ways that honor home and resident choice are endless, and they are often one of the most difficult changes to conceptualize. Meds, and sometimes even medical records can be stored inside each resident's room in properly secured drawers or cubbies. They can be stored in a central med room and distributed individually to each resident wherever they may be at the moment using a small basket or tray. They may also be stored in a stationary cabinet close to several residents' rooms, designed to look like household furniture but with the internal fixin's of a stationary med cart. The common purpose of all these options is to *eliminate* the traditional med cart and all of its related messages of institution. Protocol and systems for decentralized medication storage are covered in *Creating Home* policies and procedures.

The traditional nursing department is somewhat dominated by the MDS process. The Household Model calls for developing new systems that decentralize this process. The intent is to move the process closer to the resident, and involve all caregivers and family in a more meaningful manner. The result should be improved care and service for residents.

Because this process is a key tool for compliance, the demonstration of outcomes and reimbursement, we cannot compromise the quality of our work in this area. But think of the advantages of a household based system; the nurse completing the MDS does not have to rely on the sometimes spotty documentation of others to accurately complete the document. For example, the household nurse who dresses a wound, assists the residents with dining and walking and gives their baths, interacts with the residents frequently throughout the day. She comes to know them personally and their fears and frustrations first hand. That same nurse can complete the MDS more accurately and more efficiently.

Activities of Daily Life

In the Household Model everyone participates in the activity of life. All staff grow in their ability to contribute to the daily pleasures of the resident and life of the household. Residents and staff create the activity of life much like in a family. Residents are happier and help craft their own pursuits. Everyone's jobs become more enjoyable and meaningful, down time gets filled with quality time, productivity increases and staff satisfaction, recruitment and retention improve.

Laundry

The household physical layout should be designed to do personal laundry in the household as indicated in the next chapter. Work with your regulators to understand their expectations for maintaining infection control in your household laundry service. Some states allow the combining of different residents' personal items into one load (with specific temperature and solution requirements). Some allow the washing of residents personal linens in the household, and some the washing of household tablecloths and napkins. Some states do not. Learn quickly where your state stands,

"In the Household Model everyone participates in the activity of life. All staff grow in their ability to contribute to the daily pleasures of the resident and life of the household."

and comply. Your residents will benefit from the process of household laundry, by smelling, feeling and hearing the comforting sounds and smells of laundry in process. Also, remember to cross train closely. Never assume all staff know not to wash wool or leather, or not to mix a new red sweatshirt with white socks.

Human Resources

Certain support functions will most likely not be changed much prior to move in. But they will offer unlimited opportunities for decentralization once the household teams have conquered the delivery of direct care and resident services in the households.

Human Resources is one of those systems. Plan to decentralize HR functions, but only once everyone has settled into the new households. Ultimately, household teams will grow to play a central role in hiring, orienting, training, scheduling and even in disciplining and terminating their members; but only with coaches and support of the Community Mentor or other mentor trained in Human Resources. Before taking on these new roles, the household teams must be trained and mentored. They need to be skilled and comfortable with their role as trainers and teachers as new team members come on board. They need to be able to see potential in others, as well as to accept their own limitations. Only then are they ready to participate actively in hiring, orienting, etc. The most powerful change yet will come when the team adds residents to their HR team. There is no better way to understand how an applicant relates to a resident than to observe them in the hiring process, particularly if the resident has physical or cognitive challenges.

Managing Household Budgets

Over time, it is possible to decentralize the functions of budgeting and fiscal planning, but like HR, implement once the dust has settled. Start the process with a "mad money" budget line item. Give each household a token amount of money (from dietary or activities or the administrator's rainy day fund) to spend monthly as they choose, but only in ways the residents have requested through learning circle or other discussions. These are not to be employee choices, but household choices that focus on residents' wishes. Perhaps it will be used to order pizza or Chinese food, take a bus ride, purchase oil paints – whatever. The household's mad money may be as little or as much as you can designate, but let the household spend it freely, without oversight from others, except for the

> "Over time, it is possible to decentralize the functions of budgeting and fiscal planning, but like HR, implement once the dust has settled. Start the process with a 'mad money' budget line item."

boundaries previously established at the onset. As the household team matures, they can evolve to fully participate in budget preparation and management.

A Household Coordinator recalls the evolution of the household budget: "The first year I was given a budget for "mad money" and provided the amount of hours we were to schedule during a pay period. In the second year, we were involved in staffing hours and learned how to manage the labor budget payroll to payroll. By the third year, we helped develop the revenue and expense budget for the house and negotiated it with management."

Culture Develops Through Behaviors and Competencies

An integrated and household based human resources system is necessary to strengthen the organizational culture and sustain the deep and systemic change.

Basic values and competencies are utilized throughout the organization in all of its decisions; and throughout the work life of the employee – from the inquiry about a job to exiting at a later date. Operative values are based on values of the organization, and through careful extrapolation, actually define the behaviors needed and expected.

Start by figuring out what's needed in the household to create the opportunities for all aspects of daily life – good clinical care, emotionally satisfying and physically nurturing foods and mealtimes, pleasurable activities and pursuits, meaningful and enjoyable relationships – in other words, good living every day.

Then begin to identify the knowledge and skills that are needed to put all of that together, and from that, the actual behaviors and attitudes that staff need to exhibit. These groupings of knowledge, skills, behaviors and attitudes are called "competencies." And so ask, "What are the competencies needed to maintain a functioning, healthy household where good life can happen?"

Once this is thought through (in highly involved teams of staff and residents), define each competency minutely by what can be measured and seen. Everyone in the organization comes to know these competencies. Individuals and teams work to grow in these competencies.

We use the term "integrated human resource system" to clarify that competencies will be defined and articulated and then utilized in all

"Operative values are based on values of the organization, and through careful extrapolation, actually define the behaviors needed and expected."

human resource functions:

- to measure applicants during selection;
- to educate new hires during orientation;
- to continuously develop leadership;
- to establish an individualized development plan;
- to encourage appropriate performance;
- to strengthen customer relationships through clear understanding;
- to mentor and coach others;
- and to serve as standards for team decision-making.

Competencies actually become the career ladders for growth in the emerging organization. They are a pathway for personal growth of every staff person - and that in turn supports the growth of the household.

ORGANIZATIONAL

Provoke the System

Embrace Chaos

We Develop

We Implement Change

Org. Becomes Ever Learning

Systems Approach Guides Development

You are creating a living system, a dynamic system to replace the task based system represented in the institution. The institution uses procedures to reduce the range of possibilities so that the institution can be assured of the outcomes. However, this system doesn't work well to foster growth and change much less produce desired outcomes. A living system shakes up the possibilities, but you must plan to more consciously move everything in sync so that nothing falls between the cracks when the shifts occur. In a living system, as one system moves, all other systems must shift and adjust. A living system is responsive to individual need, and flows accordingly. You will continually be challenged to move with the shifts, and to consider the effects on everything else.

How do you monitor the quality of this living, shifting system? By determining the ability of the system to meet the need of every resident. Resident choice drives system change, and even the smallest of resident choices can touch every system in the household. Remember that as everything shifts and changes, you must assure regulatory compliance or something will fall through the cracks.

"You will continually be challenged to move with shifts, and to consider the effects on everything else."

"Resident choice drives system change, and even the smallest of resident choices can touch every system in the household."

WE IMPLEMENT THE CHANGE, ENERGIZED CHAOS ERUPTS

This is a time of celebration and satisfaction for all, as well as the time to resist any and all temptations to go back to the old way.

Focus first on where you are, what is now and what is next. Save time later to reflect individually and as a team on what might come later, and

ORGANIZATIONAL

Provoke the System

Embrace Chaos

We Develop

We Implement Change

Org. Becomes Ever Learning

on what might be better accomplished with a slight tweak in the system. It won't be just right and certainly not perfect the first time around, but remember that you are a learning organization; learn from the past and the present to create your own most desired future.

Recognize that implementation happens not just at move in, but minute by minute, hour by hour, day by day for years to come. Every time you recommit to the Essential Elements and your organization's values; every time you respond to an elder's need or desire in an individualized way; every time you experience the enhanced contribution of a staff person no longer constrained by the traditional boundaries of department or task, you are continuing to implement deep and significant change.

Celebrate deep satisfaction with every small step forward, and remember to make it community-wide when opportunities present themselves. At the same time, give yourself and others permission to reflect and re-challenge. Perhaps you will suffer small steps back toward traditional thinking, but hold firm that your actions continue to move the organization forward. Remember the power of stories, and the power of the learning circle. Remember the collective conscience and power of team decision making. Use them all to celebrate and to sustain.

THE ORGANIZATION BECOMES EVERLEARNING

Yours is a learning organization. Counting on ever-changing needs and circumstances replaces counting on things always being the same. Looking back, it may seem strange that you ever worked in a traditional long-term care environment. Elders' needs and desires are ever-changing. So too, by its very nature, is the Household Model. As people, our likes and dislikes change. Maybe we sleep in a little more during winter or stay up later in summer. Maybe we discover a delicious new hot chocolate that we begin having routinely before bed. Then, maybe after drinking it so often we don't want it as much as before. Such is the tide of creating the good life with elders - the shared vision of home by and for the elders.

The organizational culture and character self-perpetuates in an upward spiral of discovery, learning, adjustments and renewal. In carrying out the vision, you seek to create a cycle of enthusiasm, communication and clarity, which in turn builds momentum. This process requires some risk-taking and experimentation. It is not about performing a certain task particularly well, but whether the task is consistent with the vision and should continue to be performed at all. It is not about what is easy or sure-fire. If the elders' best interest is at heart, it is worth trying.

"It won't be just right and certainly not perfect the first time around, but remember that you are a learning organization; learn from the past and the present to create your own most desired future."

"Counting on ever-changing needs and circumstances replaces counting on things always being the same."

"The organizational culture and character self-perpetuates in an upward spiral of discovery, learning, adjustments and renewal."

Once again we look to Senge in *The Fifth Discipline*, "Building an organization where it is safe for people to create visions, where inquiry and commitment to the truth are the norm and challenging the status quo is expected – especially when the status quo includes obscuring aspects of current reality that people seek to avoid." In this sense, cohabitation with creative chaos becomes the desired norm. Why do we strive for chaos over status quo? Or, even make chaos the status quo? Because there are more possibilities in chaos. Many creative and successful people we've known over the years have incredibly messy desks or offices. Because generally our society embraces status quo, most of us think there is something wrong with a messy desk. However, like these people's minds, their desks are places where anything can happen. No idea or paper is filed in one specific place, pigeon holed for one stayed purpose only. Ideas and papers can move, change and be looked at in different ways. Energy is spent finding the possibilities contained within them instead of arranging them in an orderly fashion. These people do not work well with a clean desk. For them, chaos is *the* way.

The organization, like a messy desk, like our newly open minds, is responsive and fluid. It has permeable edges that absorb what it needs to stay viable. In ten years, as things change, as the residents and staff change, it may look different, but it will still be the *elders'* place.

It is by normalizing creative chaos that the organization becomes ever learning. Learning becomes part of everyone's day-to-day job. People must continually practice the art of learning, growing and creating. To be good at anything requires practice. And then, as we become skilled, we must continue practicing to maintain our skill. This is how we will embrace the reality and normalcy of life in our households and leave the institution behind.

"Why do we strive for chaos over status quo? Or, even make chaos the status quo? Because there are more possibilities in chaos."

"It is by normalizing creative chaos that the organization becomes ever learning."

chapter 10
Environmental Transformation

contributing co-authors: Migette Kaup and Jeff Anderzohn

"Home is the most popular and will be
the most enduring of all earthly establishments."
- Channing Pollock

HOME OR HALLWAY – THE DEBATE BEGINS

Institutional Design Is Challenged

By the time your organization is ready to determine how to approach designing the physical environment, the Steering and Action Teams should be well along the road of spreading and deepening the transformational journey.

This chapter assumes organizational and leadership changes are already happening and new ways of thinking are taking root. Individuals throughout the organization are taking responsibility for self-transformation, and stories of personal growth and epiphanies are circulating. At this juncture, your journey has moved well beyond the passion of a single leader or a small group of change agents to become an organization-wide conversation and creation process. Internal and external stakeholders are showing strong signs of integrated alignment around the vision of resident-directed service within the Household Model.

While some are still unsure of how it *really* will be and feel, staff is generally rallied around the concept of creating home, decentralized, self-led teams, pleasant work environments and increased meaning and purpose for those who live and work there.

By now, the collective organization clearly realizes residents have basic rights it must address (the normalcy of daily life in a household community, choice and the opportunity to pursue individual interests and direct their own lives). The organization has adopted strong values emphasizing the sanctity of each resident's home – values its caregivers strive to ensure are lived out.

You have challenged yourselves to let go of the institutional design. Your organization is attracted to the Household Model, and your frequent high involvement conversations have shifted the organizational mindset from institution to home. The remaining questions are: Can we afford to do it? Will we have hallway, or will we have home?

Discordance Between Household and Traditional Operating Model Design

It is very important to take stock of your progress with organizational change. There is an obvious and close partnership between the physical environment and the services delivered. These two dimensions push and pull upon each other constantly. Changing the environment is the easy part. It may take considerable time and money, but it's fun and there's immediate gratification. Positive outcomes become verifiably visible on paper as concepts begin taking shape.

It is critically important to ensure personal, leadership and organizational transformation processes as outlined in the Norton-Shields Change Matrix are in tandem with a conceived building or retrofit project. Otherwise, it is easy to transform only the physical environment and convince yourself you've made an organizational change. Once a building or retrofit project begins, it also is tempting to say, "We'll wait until after it's built and make the organizational changes when we move in."

The problem is, once you take the old world into the new environment you've let the wolf through the door, and it is difficult to send it packing. Leave bad habits and old mindsets in the old environment. Embrace the new culture and carry it across the threshold of the new households.

The household design and how life is lived within it must be in accord to truly achieve and sustain the Household Model. However, if you have to choose between changing your organization and creating a pretty space, choose the former. One thing worse than traditional nursing home service in a traditionally designed building is traditional nursing home service in a building designed as a Household Model. It simply doesn't work. Having a built environment like home without the reality of home only magnifies the ills of the traditional system. More importantly, the very nature of the Household Model's physical design is at odds with traditional staffing patterns and methodologies.

Do or Die

Truth is, the traditional nursing home model is fast approaching a long overdue death. You can either "save" money while driving the organization down a death spiral, or pull together the resources needed to invest in your future.

Traditional nursing home buildings continue to age and depreciate. If you tabulate the expense of enabling the existing physical environment through another life cycle, you likely will be surprised at the capital resources needed to simply maintain the status quo. Comparing that tabulation with the costs of a new or retrofitted household environment may show capital dollars can be utilized more wisely than you thought.

Put bluntly, if you don't physically (and culturally) reinvent your organization, a competitor will likely beat you to the punch. The winds of change are gathering. The long-term care establishment, notorious for remaining static, is rapidly being surrounded by a spiral of change. It is a mistake to think past and present inertia will continue. New ways are

"You can either 'save' money while driving the organization down a death spiral or pull together the resources needed to invest in your future."

unfolding that will take the marketplace by storm. In the decade ahead, new physical and organizational designs will be all around you.

(Authors' Side note: A surprising number of providers continue to build traditional facilities. The only thing more dangerous economically than an old, depreciated, traditional nursing home competing with a neighboring Household Model is a new, un-depreciated, mortgaged, traditional facility competing with a neighboring Household Model.)

Not only is the physical environment a major component in the lifestyle of the people who live within it; it is a very visible aspect of how the market perceives your organization. It is the first signal to those who compare your services with other nursing homes. The Household Model clearly stands apart. The question is who is going to offer it, you or your competitor? One day, even if you make the right decision, it will be both. Then it will be a matter of who does it better.

Admittedly, we push this point rather strongly. However, we have seen many instances where staff and residents rally around a vision of the Household Model, only to have it unnecessarily stunted because scarcity thinking led the ownership to limit capital investment. Instead of creating a new future, they put a bandage on the rising hopes of the organization by eliminating the nurses' station, putting in plants or creating a buffet. These interventions moderately improve the status quo, but they are not a good end game.

Will Abundance or Scarcity Shape the Possibilities?

As the vision of a resident-directed, decentralized organizational culture begins to take shape in the minds and hearts of planners, mental images of the home environment are stirred. Hunger for physical changes usually becomes evident as planning for transformation advances.

This is when you arrive at a fork in the road. One road takes the dream toward reality. The other is a dead-end where the dream bumps against real or perceived resource limitations. It is very important that the Administrator (we use this term to include the senior decision maker whether it be the owner, CEO, President, etc.) carefully considers the available *and* potential resources needed to make the physical changes that must accompany full fruition of the Household Model.

Scarcity Thinking

The traditional nursing home model has created a mindset of

"It is a mistake to think past and present inertia will remain. New ways are unfolding that will take the marketplace by storm."

"The physical environment is not only a major component in the lifestyle of people who live within it; it is a very visible aspect of how the market perceives your organization."

scarcity thinking. We too often assume "we can't" as a matter or course. Consequently, we have developed a culture of "make do with what we've got."

We learn to pinch pennies, and often do not invest in formally determining our real potential. We mistakenly think we are good stewards if we don't spend money. We measure our effectiveness by how much we avoid spending, even if we truly need to spend. We authors have seen, time and time again, administrators who set out to explore project feasibility only to be scared off when consultants quote their day rates. We must spend money to make money, but many of us in long-term care can't get over the hump of scarcity thinking. As the saying goes, we are "pennywise and pound-foolish" without realizing how much it limits our future.

When long-term care administrators converse, the talk is frequently about limitations, constraints and struggle. True, resources are often scarce but our outlook cannot be. Our sense of possibility must be filtered through an outlook of abundance. Our resources are scarce *because* our outlook is scarce. It can be difficult to recognize this cause-and-effect relationship.

The perception of available resources is often inaccurate. In our work around the country, we authors have talked with hundreds of organizational leaders who had jumped to a unilateral decision of "we can't afford it." But upon questioning them, we learned they hadn't formally tested their assumptions.

Often, decision makers cannot see beyond their informal estimates of the initial cost of physical construction or retrofitting. Their financial analysis does not go beyond calculating estimated construction costs and monthly payments necessary to pay down additional debt. Their conclusions are based only on existing revenues and expenses. Rarely calculated are potential income, census increases and measurable resident/staff quality of life improvements.

When contemplating large-scale physical plant changes or new construction, many administrators say, "We would like to do the Household Model, but can't afford it. We're only going to make small changes."

Sometimes they are merely afraid of wholesale change and hide behind the "we can't" curtain. But most times, their habit of scarcity thinking leads them to believe they can't afford plant changes or replacements involving significant capital investment.

On the other hand, some do formal analysis and rightfully conclude they cannot afford the capital required. They take the important step of investigating and substantiating. But while they may go beyond the efforts

"It is true that resources are often scarce, but our outlook cannot be."

of their counterparts, many stop too soon instead of investigating merger/acquisition potential or other creative options in their market area.

If you truly can't afford the capital, in most cases it means your organization has a limited lifespan. Our industry generally is not ready to openly acknowledge this reality, but it is true nonetheless. Merging with another organization can infuse life into both and may provide leverage to create a sound future that includes progressive alternatives like the Household Model.

The main thing is, do a thorough and professional analysis of your options before closing the door to your potential.

ALIGNMENT OF VISION AND RESOURCES BEGINS

Prefeasibility Analysis May Open Doors You Haven't Thought Possible

Before you limit your organization's future, we strongly suggest you invest in project pre-feasibility forecasting to help determine what truly is financially possible – whether you can do only limited improvements or accomplish the Household Model.

Administrators many times will first engage an architect to begin programming and design and, in effect, use them as the primary instrument to determine if a project is even feasible. This can be a *very* expensive approach. It is very important to evaluate your existing operational health and translate your vision into budget parameters *before* beginning the design process. Prefeasibility analysis is the preliminary stage of establishing early measures and indicators of project feasibility before engaging expensive development professionals in the design process.

If you are able to do the Household Model, the pre-feasibility study will further indicate if you are able to retrofit your existing plant or build new households from the ground up. Both are very desirable options.

If only limited improvements are feasible, the Household Model is not possible but other culture change advancements clearly are. Alternative models with more gradualist philosophies should be fully explored to determine the best fit for your organization. Completing the pre-feasibility study helps determine not only the extent of your ability to infuse capital into the organization, but also which model of change you can work toward.

"Administrators many times will first engage an architect to begin programming and design and, in effect, use them as the primary instrument to determine if a project is even feasible. This can be a **very** expensive approach."

"Prefeasibility analysis is the preliminary stage of establishing early measures and indicators of project feasibility before engaging expensive development professionals in the design process."

But Where Do We Start?

Assessing current capital in terms of human, environmental and financial resources is one of the first steps in pre-feasibility inquiry. Until these three are balanced, or at least seem to be moving toward balance, detractors will try to throw the project off track.

Financial professionals can sit down with you and your staff to create a pre-feasibility forecast framework and model. While no two nursing homes are exactly alike, there are many benchmarks to use for exploring potential outcomes resulting from the changes you are planning. The forecast should factor in the experience and results of others who have transformed to the Household Model.

Nursing homes often have what traditional providers refer to as "empty beds" and thus think they can't afford to invest in environmental improvement. Transforming your organization to the Household Model dramatically increases the likelihood you will be full with a waiting list, and that likelihood can significantly impact your project's feasibility at the onset. It is a factor often overlooked. Consequently, we emphasize this piece of the puzzle in the financial forecast.

Engaging Pre-feasibility Professionals

To determine the level of environmental change you can make with the resources available, you need to engage an architect, a financial forecaster and possibly a market feasibility firm at the initial exploratory stage. Engaging design and financial professionals at the beginning will provide a more accurate forecast of project costs based on the Household Model's conceptual physical and organizational design.

You may also want to engage a Household Model consultant, if you haven't already, at this phase to ensure all design and culture-related assumptions are appropriate and integrated. Household Model consultants usually have good general knowledge of the operational, cultural and physical design elements, have been involved in previous projects and can help your pre-feasibility team further adapt to the new concept. Significantly and simultaneously changing your physical and organizational design can feel overwhelming, so it is very important to have sufficient expertise and support on the front end of the project.

These professionals should be part of a team to help articulate your fundamental concepts and establish the project scope and budget. While the pre-feasibility consultants may or may not be the same team who take your project through design onto construction, it is helpful if they all have household design and forecasting experience to ensure your assumptions are solid. They will be instrumental in making sure you factor in everything

"Transforming your organization to the Household Model dramatically increases the likelihood you will be full with a waiting list, and thereby can significantly impact your project's feasibility at the onset."

"Significantly and simultaneously changing your physical and organizational design can feel overwhelming, so it is very important to have sufficient expertise and support on the front end of the project."

necessary to produce a valid forecast. If you have difficulty locating such a firm, contact providers who you know have implemented the Household Model. They can likely direct you to qualified candidates.

Architectural Pre-feasibility

At the pre-feasibility stage, you are not committing to a design but merely articulating your conceptual and programmatic goals. Nor are you necessarily committed to continuing with the architect or financial consultants past the pre-feasibility inquiry. But if you do continue with them, they may comprise an engaged and knowledgeable team at the outset of the design and development process. You have to determine if the team that is good at forecasting is also good at design and project management. However, the architect should be fitting the plan to *your* vision, not the other way around.

The pre-feasibility architect can establish the square footages and construction costs within a reasonable range once concepts are articulated. This information is valuable to your financial consultant(s) who can help you create a forecast model that captures construction and related project costs, operating revenues and expenses, and other variables needed as indicators of project feasibility.

It is also important to factor in "phasing" if it applies to your situation. Retrofit projects are usually phased because it is necessary to move people to new housing in stages as the project moves forward. You are usually able to complete one house or one section of a house at a time, move residents in, and then begin retrofitting another. Phasing time and cost implications should not be overlooked during the pre-feasibility stage.

Market Pre-feasibility Analysis

Engaging a marketing firm to complete a demographic/competitive analysis will give you a sense of the potential to add services and increase revenues. It will reveal the need to investigate merger and acquisition possibilities if you lack a strong demographic base (or for other reasons) and the characteristics of your market place, including what the market will bear and the impact of competitors.

The analysis will also show the impact and probability of penetrating into secondary and tertiary markets. Depending on the form of financing, a formal market study may later be required by your funding source (lender, investor or underwriter). While that may or may not be the case in your situation, we strongly recommend you consider a thorough market study at the pre-feasibility phase whether it is required or not. A comprehensive,

"The pre-feasibility architect can establish the square footages and construction costs within a reasonable range once concepts are articulated. This information is valuable to your financial consultant(s) who can help you create a forecast model."

"Engaging a marketing firm to complete a demographic/ competitive analysis will give you a sense of the potential to add services and increase revenues."

demographic and competitive market analysis will give you solid footing to move forward with your project in a responsible and grounded way. Audit firms typically either have professionals onboard who do such studies, or can readily refer you to them. Seasoned underwriters can also help you locate experienced market study firms.

Often nursing home providers think only in terms of "our market is our town," or the immediate catchment area (known as the primary market). But the community is full of people with aging parents living elsewhere. This tertiary market is commonly overlooked. The arrival of the Household Model will change many relationships between children residing in your community and their parents who live somewhere else. Adult children are more likely to invite parents to move to their community if they clearly see it would significantly improve their parents' lives. As it is, adult children frequently hesitate to push for a move if it is just from one nursing home to another. The benefits for parents in remaining close to their friends or in a familiar community often outweigh moving. But a new and dramatically better alternative often shifts the scales. Consequently, your relationship with your market will likely broaden considerably with the Household Model.

Changing to the Household Model may determine the difference between having empty rooms and accommodations and being full with a waiting list. The potential of the Household Model to penetrate the primary, secondary and tertiary markets needs to be thoroughly estimated, justified and included in the pre-feasibility forecast.

Bucking Conventional Wisdom Within the Market/Demographic Analysis

Nursing home census reflect declining trends across the country, leading to the prevailing wisdom that it is not generally advisable to build additional nursing home accommodations. We challenge that line of thinking. While there is little question regarding the overall trends, emerging data indicates the market is quite attracted to the Household Model, and transfers from other facilities are commonplace.

If no other Household Model organizations are in your primary or secondary markets, you can make a solid case for adding accommodation capacity to your Household Model design as a way to increase the feasibility of your project. In most cases this involves working the Certificate of Need process, which is often difficult. Once completed, your new product offering will shine in the marketplace. While there is no question the

"A comprehensive demographic/competitive market analysis will give you the solid footing to move forward with your project in a responsible and grounded way."

number of nursing homes will decrease in the coming decade, those that reposition themselves stand a much larger chance of not just surviving but flourishing.

Market analysis can illuminate the demographic trends in your area and provide census information within your marketplace. It also will help you see merger and acquisition potentials more clearly. This is important to investigate because merger and closure of one facility (or both if you build new households) not only increases your ability to add new accommodations; it will also ensure accelerating census stabilization, in turn strengthening financial feasibility. In addition, this can simplify the Certificate of Need process.

While a pre-feasibility study will give you a sense of what can be accomplished with your available resources, you still need to determine the environmental transformation goals and how they support the policy and operational changes you put into place. You need what architects and designers call a building program, or – if your project warrants it – a master plan. The organizational transformation goals need to be articulated, and then merged with and supported by the building's physical design.

From here the scope of the project can be determined, which in turn leads to the next level of planning operational budgets, financial feasibility and environmental design.

Making the Decision – Retrofit or Build

Once you have used your existing financial model to forecast the costs of construction, staffing and organizational restructuring, you can determine the level of environmental changes your facility is ready to make. The pre-feasibility process should tell you which of the two Household Model approaches are possible.

You don't truly arrive at this decision-making point until you complete the pre-feasibility inquiry. An alignment in your values, organizational structure, operational behaviors and environment begins to be evident, and you begin to realistically understand what you can accomplish.

The sense of scarcity is likely beginning to be replaced by an outlook of abundance. Rather than, "*Can* we afford to do it," the question now is "*Which* can we afford?"

There are two environmental options for creating the Household Model: renovate and/or build. If you can't or don't prefer to abandon your existing facility, it can be retrofitted into multiple houses, often within the

"While there is no question the number of nursing homes will decrease in the coming decade, those that reposition themselves stand a much larger chance of not just surviving but flourishing."

envelope of the existing building. If you start anew, you have the luxury of beginning with a blank piece of paper.

In either option, design should be in harmony with the Essential Elements of the Household Model as outlined in Chapter Four, and with the household anatomy and design principles offered in this chapter.

Option 1: Remodel an existing (traditional) nursing home into households

Fortunately, old institutional building designs are perfect for converting into the Household Model. If pre-feasibility analysis indicates renovation is your most financially viable approach, you will likely have solid options for conversion. Renovation may require some rethinking of how space is used to create home. Start the environmental planning analysis by using a basic floor plan (a copy of the fire evacuation plan will work) to label every room and space. Look at the words you've used to describe the spaces and their current functions and ask, "Would I find these rooms in my own home?"

There are probably labeled spaces that have no residential meaning or usage. Discuss which should be converted into residential living areas. Determine how open social spaces can be retrofitted to fit the Household Model.

Next, analyze the number and types of privacy zones you find on the plan by looking for four levels of activity: public, semi-public, semi-private and private. Color-coding your plan is a powerful way to understand where conflicts lie in providing residential privacy. An over abundance of one color (particularly the color for "public") means you should evaluate patterns of resident circulation, activity and social interaction for changes that could enhance privacy.

Think of each hallway as a future household. Entrances and living spaces will need to be created or reorganized for each new house. You will not want to simply share with other households the existing larger rooms where everyone currently gathers. Part of the building that has a large room may have to be transformed into resident bedrooms, while resident bedrooms along hallways with no common spaces may need to be converted to social space. This allows for a front door, foyer, living room, dining room and kitchen for each house. In this case, "robbing Peter to pay Paul" is a sound strategy.

Remember, you are looking for opportunities to make houses out of hallways and a few large rooms. It will be easier than you think to conceptualize a living room, dining room, kitchen and other areas integrated and connected to a specific number of bedrooms. Minor new

"Our old institutional building designs are perfect candidates for conversion to the Household Model"

Meadowlark Hill – Health Care Remodel – Spatial Hierarchy Before and After
Assessment of Space and Graphics developed by Migette L. Kaup, Kansas State University

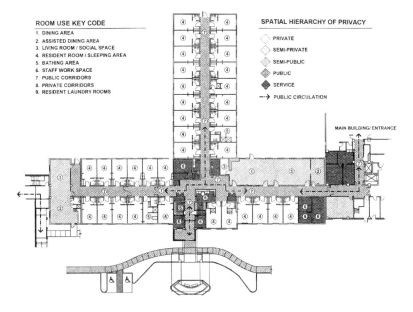

Figure No. 1 – Health Care Plan before Remodel

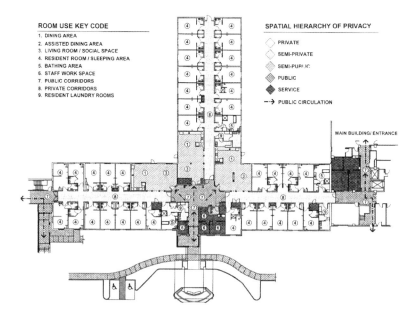

Figure No. 2 – Health Care Plan after Remodel

Example of traditional "T-Shaped" building with common spatial arrangements that do not support residential privacy

construction (i.e. adding on rooms) may also figure into your plans, and may allow you to expand living/dining rooms or reconfigure/add private bedrooms.

Decentralizing a common space to create several smaller household rooms brings excitement and increased commitment once you clearly see how to do it in the existing building.

Plan to carefully review with your architect all viable options within the existing plant. Once engaged, your architect can help identify and work around limitations. Look for changes that will most dramatically impact the elders' quality of life while supporting your operational and organizational transformation.

Option 2: Start From Scratch – New Construction

If you have resources to build new households rather than renovating an existing structure, you can achieve a greater dimension of the Household Model. The scope of your project must be carefully defined. You will need to review with the project architect the level of construction quality you expect. Construction costs are impacted by three major variables; quantity (size/scale of the project), quality (impacting the aesthetic character and how well materials will hold up over time) and time (the speed of construction and schedules that must be met. If phasing is involved, it will affect time.) New construction enables you to avoid the constraints of an existing building. You have an empty canvas with paintbrush in hand!

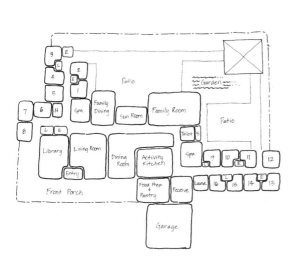
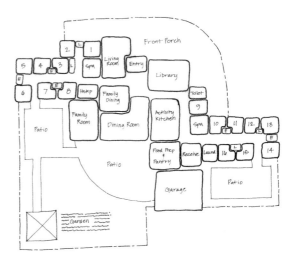

Conceptual arrangement of spaces in a new household model

ENGAGE PARTNERS IN DESIGN

Anchor Your Vision Before Engaging the Development Team

Now that you are in the mindset of creating home in a literal way, the fundamental design principles that interconnect with the cultural framework of the Household Model must be clear in your mind before engaging your architect for actual design and other development team members. Otherwise, it is common for providers to engage an architect and rely too heavily on the design firm's vision. Architects often report a "do it for me" culture in provider/designer relationships. This can be, and often is, lethal to a project.

As you contemplate assembling a development team with people outside of your organization, be aware that each player may see him or herself as the centerpiece of the team. They may not be accustomed to being part of a true team effort. It also is not uncommon for development team members to do their individual piece in a silo without clearly understanding the project vision or the efforts of other team members. Combine this with a provider mentality of "do it for me," and you have a project in trouble. Consequently, you, as the provider, must clearly position yourself to lead the group. (Having a developer or development consultant can make this job easier, but you must ensure the developer/consultant is in total sync with your vision. It is not unusual for a developer's approach to collide with the non-traditional Household Model.)

Specifically, you are ill advised to rely on the architect's offering without first clearly articulating your vision. In long-term care, we are famous for being driven by our design and development teams instead of instilling a reciprocal creation partnership into the development process. You need to be the primary source of vision for the architect as well as for the other development team members.

To help prepare for assembling your development team, the next few pages are intended to ground you in the fundamental philosophies, principles and characteristics of the Household Model as it relates to the building. This, along with the Essential Elements and the "Norton-Shields Change Matrix" should ground your organization in the Household Model as you begin engaging the development team.

"We are famous for being driven by our design and development teams instead of instilling a reciprocal creation partnership."

Rethinking the Role of Place – What Does It Mean To Have A Home?

When the time arrives to engage the development team, articulating your vision will help the design team ensure the physical elements of the project envelop the desired organizational, cultural and operational changes.

The purpose is to create home with and for those who live there. The term "home" is often associated with a place central to our lives and may bring about images of a building or features of a space. The significance of the word, however, reaches beyond simple imagery. Homes are territories used to establish boundaries between families, the outside world and us; they guard privacy and the very character of our lives.

Clare Cooper Marcus says in her article, *Self-identity and the Home*, "Home can be a room or dwelling to which we return every day; it can also be a state of mind. To feel 'at home' is to feel comfortable, at ease, relaxed, perhaps surrounded by those few who truly understand or care for us. To be homeless is not only to be deprived of basic shelter; it is to be stripped of any place in the world where one can truly feel 'at home.'"

Most of us are fortunate enough to live in homes our entire lives. The behaviors associated with sharing a house have been a part of our identity since we could walk and talk. We know how to behave through our interactions with those in and outside of our family as it relates to our home; we didn't learn it in a classroom. We didn't have to wait until the first day of school to learn things like "when mom's in the tub, don't open the bathroom door; she wants her privacy."

We learn to respect privacy and other social boundaries of the people we live with by interacting with them, watching their behaviors and relating those behaviors within different spaces in the home environment. It has been so long since we learned these lessons, however, their significance may now seem trivial. We respond intuitively without much conscious thought about how our life activities and observed boundaries relate to physical and personal space.

We must take great care to bring these unconscious customs to the conscious level as we begin planning the sanctuary where people will live. It's not that we don't know already; the problem is we know at such a deep level we don't realize we possess it. Most times we automatically, without thinking about it, observe the most sacred of social agreements as it relates to behavior with others in our own home and theirs. Consequently, we are often not mindful to ensure our elders have what we take for granted every day of our lives. The challenge is to be mindful of those customs as you plan a new home for elders and ensure the house reflects the values and life patterns of normal everyday living.

It's a very easy concept. Yet it is a seemingly difficult one for the long-term care community to grasp: We're building home. It's just that simple.

Traditional nursing home designs do not lend themselves to the

"It's a very easy concept. Yet it is a seemingly difficult one for the long-term care community to grasp. We're building home. It's just that simple."

patterns of residential lifestyles. When thinking about privacy in nursing homes, we have focused on procedures, staff efficiency and resident movement. Public hallways pass by bedrooms – spaces considered among the most private in a residential home.

Nursing home designs have not focused on patterns of home life that support intuitive behaviors of privacy and individual pursuits. Therefore the experience of privacy for nursing home residents is often non-existent. Since the goal of the Household Model is to replace the institutional experience with one of home, you need to support residential privacy through the architectural design. Simply adding familiar residential imagery may create a home-like setting, but will not address the deeper issues. "Home" means, "This is where you live," not "Pretend this is your home."

To reach this point, we must focus on the essential details that capture the fundamental meaning of home. We can do so by understanding how the spaces of nursing homes can be designed and arranged to support attitudes and behaviors that are natural within a family and home setting.

To effectively create a home experience, attention to the arrangement of spaces and the sequential nature of circulation between rooms must be carefully considered. The cueing we receive from features in a building sends a powerful message. A front door implies, for example, that we should request permission to enter. To barge into someone's house unannounced and uninvited would typically be met with a negative reaction from the homeowner. Inside the home there are additional signals for behavior through the placement of walls, doors, lighting, cabinetry, appliances and furnishings.

Scale – Small Versus Large Spaces: What Are the Impacts on Perception?

Another challenge is the size of space and deciding how to use it effectively. Most traditional nursing homes have one large room where a majority of activities occur including meals, crafts, television, worship services and other large group activities. Staff may be open to adding residential touches to these rooms, but are often reluctant to exchange these spaces for smaller ones because the multipurpose room is a major component in the life of the nursing home. Staff often say, "Oh, we can't make that smaller, we won't be able to get everyone in here for the holiday program!"

Should we design the spaces around one or two days of the year, or do we design for the other 363 days? Shouldn't we design for daily living, which should include space for small groups that support family and one-on-one personal connections?

Working with elders every day teaches us that residents with vision or hearing loss function better when information is close to them. We bend down to make eye contact and speak at a close range so a resident can see, hear and respond. A large room brings with it lots of auditory and visual stimulation. Much of this arrives as muddled noise to elders, who have difficulty accurately separating out the information that is important to them. With so much going on, a resident who doesn't see or hear well is prevented from receiving and responding to quality information. Because no one complains, it seems we assume these functional needs disappear when the children's choir comes at holiday time, or when a large group of residents eat together in a big space.

Ideally, the household has a variety of spaces and rooms where people gather. Picture a large social gathering in your home, and you likely will conjure up images of guests conversing with one another in rooms throughout the house. Often, if the weather permits, there is overflow into the screened-in porch, deck or patio. Sometimes we set up tables and a string of lights up in the yard. This is the mindset suggested by the Household Model.

Design Principles for the Household Model

Consider using the following design principles as your organization formulates its vision of the Household Model:

Principle 1: Seek normalcy in all things.

Bringing residential patterns of life into a skilled care setting means letting go of institutional thinking. This impacts every decision we make about the environmental features in the home. Eliminate the institutional sterility. As you make design choices, once again, use Bump's Law. Ask: What does the resident want? How did the resident do it at home? How do we do it at home? How should we do it here? If what you are planning doesn't pass the Bump test, rethink it. It must look, feel, smell and function as a true home we are all familiar with in our own lives.

Principle 2: Home is our sanctuary.

Home is one of our most valued possessions. It reflects who we are and our relationships with people around us. There must be personalized spaces within the household for both the individual and the collective

"Seek normalcy in all things"

"Home is our sanctuary."

family. Household residents should decide what is to be included in their surroundings, thus enabling them to internalize the environment as their home.

The design should include intimate and private spaces that allow residents to live out their individual pursuits. A comfortable chair with a pole lamp and a side table near bookshelves, for example, may be a space for one who likes to read; a separate game room or a game table in the library for playing cards or board games or writing letters; comfortable patio furniture for sitting out and enjoying the sunshine.

We all recognize the feeling of sanctuary within our own homes. As we have previously shared, we feel it most when we return from a long trip and first walk through the door and let out that audible sigh like we do only when arriving home. This is the feeling we must create in the Household Model.

The interior design of a house is an important dimension that affects how elders perceive things around them. Colors must have appropriate contrasts that are tasteful and comfortable in their palette. A balance between darker and lighter colors is important, but colors that are too vibrant, trendy and quickly dated may not be a durable choice. Pastel colors, while bright and cheery, are not perceived well by aged eyes.

Upholstered furniture must meet flammability standards, but options for furniture in health care environments are expanding. Keep in mind that few of our homes have only one style of furniture. Insist on investigating style options rather than falling back on models that promote the most clinical aesthetic. Resist purchasing household furniture from nursing home suppliers unless they have significantly expanded product lines. You may wish to ask for advice from a knowledgeable interior designer with gerontological experience who can identify features of furniture styles appropriate for frail elders. Be sure the designer understands and is driven by your vision of home. Select textiles that feel soft, and finishes that convey comfort and warmth. Furnishings and finishes can have tactile qualities of home and still be safe, healthy and cleanable.

Resident pictures and personal belongings can and should be integrated with the household décor as residents wish. But often staff will bring "institutional think" into the environment with the best of intentions. It's one thing to have finger paintings grandchildren gave Grandma displayed on the kitchen fridge. That's home. Its quite another to have finger paintings from a visiting classroom lining the corridor walls and integrated with seasonal borders carefully displayed by an activity director.

That is institution.

Design Principle 3: Home is where we host our visitors.

"Home is where we host our visitors."

Family, friends and community are important throughout our lives including when we become old and frail. Elders living in the Household Model enjoy the company of loved ones as a normal part of daily life. The nature of such visits, however, should dramatically transform from those typical in a traditional nursing home. The receiving of guests should be factored into the design of home. Several small rooms (living room, main dining room, kitchen, private dining room, library/den. etc.) have the advantage of allowing multiple social interactions to occur on a small scale simultaneously throughout the house.

A daughter and her husband may visit Mom in her private bedroom while a sister has coffee with her brother at the kitchen table. Meanwhile, Grandma reads a story to her great-granddaughter in the library. A birthday luncheon happily plays out in the private dining room, and a few residents and staff watch "As the World Turns" in the living room. As people from each setting move about, perhaps stepping into the kitchen to get a couple of root beers, they stop and visit with one another. The residents, staff and visitors are all instruments in the orchestra creating the rhythm of the household. Think through how your manifestation of the Household Model can make receiving guests easy and joyful. The design of your households should foster the interactions described above.

Careful consideration must be given to amenities to enhance guest experiences, especially of little visitors to the household. Children easily get left out of the equation in settings for elders. A basket of toys, a candy jar, board and electronic games and a tricycle on the patio create connections with children and give them something additional to look forward to when visiting great-grandpa or grandma.

Design Principle 4: All homes have a front door.

"All homes have a front door."

The symbol of a home's front door is universally identifiable and understood. This is the feature of home that signals "welcome" to visitors and the division between public and private spaces. Within the design, celebrate the front door as both the implied and explicit delineation that it is. Ensure it looks like any other outside front door by adding a doorbell, mailbox, porch light and doormat – perhaps even a front porch and address numbers. Examine the feasibility of having brick or external siding even if the exterior of the household entrance is within the building. These will strengthen the message of home to all who enter. Plain and simple: It isn't a house without a front door.

"The residents, staff and visitors are all instruments in the orchestra creating the rhythm of the household."

"All homes have a kitchen."

Design Principle 5: All homes have a kitchen.

The kitchen is the heart of the home - every home around the world. People everywhere relate to the fellowship and communion around food that is born and nurtured in the kitchen. We look to the kitchen as the source of sensory stimulation – sights, sounds, smells, tastes and textures – that is important to reality orientation, memory and reflection, as well as to appetite and hydration. The kitchen is a natural place for personal interaction over the preparation of the meal or the baking of special treats. Kitchens should be designed not only as a place to for preparing food, but also for gathering and socializing. One can enjoy the moment over a cup of coffee or a snack, but just sitting quietly in the familiar environment of a family kitchen can stir memories from every stage of life: as a young child experiencing mother's baking, as a teenager with the fun of a barbeque, as a young bride with the laughs over a fallen angelfood cake, of connecting to the community by preparing a signature dessert to share with friends, as a grandfather and grand child, one baking, one licking the spoon... The obvious truth is that kitchens are necessary for preparing and serving meals, but in a home, kitchens are just as necessary between meals for building and sustaining relationships, and for nourishing the soul.

"All homes have recognizable dimensions of privacy."

Principle 6: All homes have recognizable dimensions of privacy.

Familiar home designs provide at least four basic zones of privacy through designation of specific rooms, their location and type of access provided. These levels can be identified as private, semi-private, semi-public and public. The chart below categorizes each zone, provides examples of spaces found in a traditional home and discusses the residential patterns of behavior you might expect. It is important to remember privacy does not equal isolation. Privacy means the ability to control social interactions and establish boundaries. The environment can play a significant role in achieving this principle and, at every level of environmental change, the goal should be to recapture as many of these dimensions of home and privacy as possible.

"It is important to remember that privacy does not equal isolation. Privacy means the ability to control social interactions and establish boundaries."

Zone	Examples of Spaces from Homes	Behaviors Expected
Public	Front door, front porch, foyer if separated from other social family spaces	Public domains include those actions and spaces that connect us to the broader community, such as picking up our mail or sitting on the front porch. The only real space inside the house that might be considered public is the foyer, but the boundary must be clearly articulated from the other social areas.
Semi-public	Living room, dining room, kitchen, family room, TV room, sun porch	Semi-public spaces are linked to activities including entertaining, cooking, eating and general forms of recreation such as watching TV or working on hobbies. This is where we eagerly invite our guests to make themselves comfortable.
Semi-private	Bedroom hallways, laundry room, den and home office	Semi-private spaces are associated with areas where we interact with members of the family in loosely structured ways. These spaces or rooms are where receiving guests is not a formal activity. The nature of the space and its relationship to other spaces allow users not to feel on-stage. These areas include workspaces where guests aren't invited, such as a laundry room or a home office.
Private	Bedrooms, bathing rooms, toilets	The most private activities of the home are usually associated with sleeping, bathing, grooming and toileting. We do not typically expose these activities to guests and many times limit access even to other family members. Some homes have both private and guest bath rooms.

Migette Kaup, 2003

While every home is unique in its layout and use of spaces based on the needs of the family, there is usually a public and a private side of the house. The manner in which guests are greeted and included in household activities is also fairly consistent; there are rooms that welcome and rooms where guests wouldn't go without permission. We rely on the physical features of space such as walls and doors to separate the most private areas. The arrangement of rooms and social norms of behavior cue these patterns. Without them, the privacy of the family and their relationships with others would be violated. We see evidence of these traditions in our own homes where rooms for social activities (semi-public areas) are close to entrances, while rooms for privacy are separated from guest areas.

The boy who delivers my newspaper is only 12 years old, yet he already understands the societal expectations of privacy.

When he comes to my door to collect payment, I go to my bedroom to get money from my purse. He knows it is not appropriate to cross the threshold unless invited, so he stays on the porch to await my return.

The boundaries are a bit different for Mrs. Naismith, my neighbor. When she comes to collect for the Cancer Society, she rings the doorbell and I invite her to have a seat on the living room couch while I get the money. Still, she would not think of wandering beyond the living room while I am gone.

When new friends come to my house for dinner, I invite them into the living room. "Can I get you a drink," I ask, and leave them sitting on the couch while I go into the kitchen to get refreshments.

But when old friends come over, I casually call out, "Come on in, we're in the kitchen." I tell them to grab a couple of beers from the fridge, and they offer to help me with the salad.

When my sister Chris comes over while I'm in the bedroom packing for a business trip, she yells hello as she comes in the back door. "I'm packing in the bedroom!" I holler, "I can't find my green blouse!" I look up and see her come into the bedroom and plop on my bed, telling me about her day as I continue packing. It's part of our relationship. If the paperboy tried it, we would have a problem on our hands.

The boundaries of privacy are dissolved even further – but not totally – between my spouse and me. He thinks nothing of popping into the bathroom to use the hair dryer while I'm taking a shower.

So, as with yours, the rooms in my house are arranged in a way that helps me to control my privacy.

"While every home is unique in its layout and use of spaces based on the needs of the family, there is usually a public and a private side of the house."

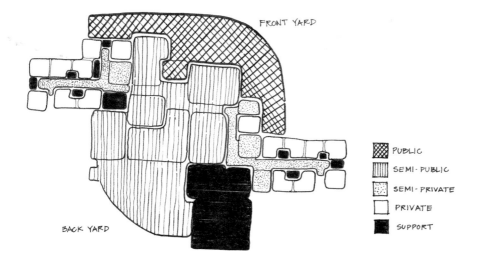

FRONT YARD

BACK YARD

PUBLIC

SEMI-PUBLIC

SEMI-PRIVATE

PRIVATE

SUPPORT

The Anatomy of a Household

If we are to identify how to achieve the fundamental principles of private and public space, we can start by looking at the components that make up a home. Each part is identifiable and uses the architecture and interior details to signify its purpose.

Entrance

The entrance to a house is a boundary that also connects us to the broader community. A front porch and a front door create a sense of residential identity.

In traditional residential architecture, the transitional zone separating the outside of the house from the sanctity of interior spaces may include a distinct foyer. This space need not be large but should be designed to reinforce those intuitively meaningful signals that guide home behavior. A closet to hang visitors' coats, an umbrella bucket or a table with a mirror are all practical signals that designate the entrance and its function in a true home.

Household Community Living Spaces

The living room is a familiar place for informal and planned socializing. It should be intimate in appearance, giving you a warm feeling just walking in to it. Incorporating bookshelves with books, a game table, or other such amenities will inspire spontaneous activity and socializing, making the best use of the space. It doesn't need to be large, the scale should be no larger that a nice sized residential living room. Moderate ceiling height will help the space feel cozy and comfortable. The television

"The entrance to a house is a boundary that also connects us to the broader community" should not be placed in such a way that it dominates life.

Additionally, it is especially desirable for each household to have other living areas for residents to use for intimate socializing, or for a comfortable quiet space to be alone yet connected to others in a familiar way. Look for opportunities to design small nooks for a couple of chairs, side table and lamp for reading, one-on-one conversations or watching television.

A room for private dining is an attractive house feature for a variety of reasons. When families or friends visit a loved one, they may prefer their own space to eat, celebrate, and converse. It is also a space that allows for other private interactions between residents, families and/or staff. The design and furnishings need to be readily identifiable as a formal or distinct dining room like we would find in any other residence.

The kitchen and dining room are the heart of the home. Mealtime is central to the culture of every household. The dining area should have a warm, comforting appearance that helps contribute to the stimulation of healthy appetites and promotes easy table conversation. The spaces and furnishings should comfortably accommodate resident movement in and out of the dining area at the time of their pleasure, as well as provide adequate space around the table(s) for a sense of private dining and conversation. The extra space required for the accommodation of wheelchairs and walker should also be taken into consideration.

Lighting is a particularly important component of creating a positive dining environment. Natural light, without glare, is generally preferred, and sometimes required by regulation. Appropriate artificial light can also create an environment that will enhance the resident's intake and independence in dining.

Food preparation in the household kitchen needs to be efficient, safe and most certainly within the regulations and fire codes for the geographic area. Still, it should be close enough to the residents that there is a strong, natural association to a residential pattern of eating. Food that arrives from a remote location may disassociate food preparation and the benefits of experiencing it from the process of having a meal. If offsite preparation is required, explore opportunities to cook or hold foods in the household kitchen in a manner that spreads the stimulating aromas throughout the household. You can also simulate the sensory stimulation with potpourrie or simply boiling cinnamon in water.

Activities centered on food preparation and food service can increase appetite and have positive outcomes for residents that include increased nutritional intake and nutritional benefits. Unfortunately, regulatory compliance in some areas may require the separation of areas and equipment for meal preparation from areas and equipment for resident activities that involve food. If carefully planned, however, these two areas can share several features and remain connected, in the form of a great room or of a pantry combining both functions in a visually open, yet physically separated space.

Fire safety and building codes will generally require some spatial separation between flame and/or heat generating appliances and other living area spaces of the household, particularly bedrooms and exit corridors. Fire safety regulations will vary not only from state to state, but also from county to county within a state, but generally any time the household kitchen has an open cooking appliance, additional fire suppression systems and/or physical separation of this appliance from exits will be needed. In fact, some interpretations of the codes may require a 20-minute firewall and/or a physical smoke partition between cooking appliances and all other living spaces. This often necessitates a "back of house" kitchen immediately behind a "front of house" kitchen, usually designated by fire officials as an "activity center." Careful planning and coordination with a committed architect or kitchen planner, combined with a powerful sense of advocacy for the resident benefits of dining at home will result in creative solutions to any perceived obstacles. Through these efforts, the residents of the household will experience the full benefits associated with the kitchen as the heart of the home.

Accept and plan that you will have more expense creating this household kitchen than one in your own home. For example, you will most likely need two refrigerators – one for residents' food so that they can come and get a drink or a snack as desired and one for the food that will be served to all residents at a meal. You may also need two dishwashers depending on your state regulations; one residential washer for resident use and one in a staff access only pantry or "back of house" kitchen that maintains higher temperatures.

Other common amenities like a sunroom or game room, depending upon your budgetary constraints, are wonderful enhancements to the physical design of the household. The challenge, if budgets don't allow specific use space, is to pack as much punch as you can into the living room, dining room, and private dining room to encourage multipurpose use.

Hallways, Bedrooms and Baths

The aforementioned spaces are all on the public side of the house. The more private spaces for bedrooms and bathing rooms are separated by passages and hallways that guests feel uncomfortable entering until properly invited.

The bedroom hallway is an important but misunderstood feature of home. Most of us don't think about its purpose. The bedroom hall, however, is designed as a privacy buffer. This space signals to guests not to trespass into more private areas of the home. It is also intended to create a visual barrier to private rooms.

Because traditional nursing homes use bedroom hallways as public thoroughfares, many who are trying to leave behind the old ways identify halls as the enemy. We visualize long, dark tunnels cluttered with equipment. For many of us, that image symbolizes the ills of the system. As a result, emerging designs often completely eliminate halls by circling resident bedrooms around social areas. This design option sacrifices residents' ability to control access to their private spaces.

Halls, although generally too long, are not the problem. The problem is how we use them and to what we connect them. In traditional nursing homes, hallways are designed to be main thoroughfares rather than privacy buffers.

When residents' bedrooms are designed to access directly to semi-public spaces like the living and dining rooms, architects may not realize egress for fire safety must still be maintained. Open areas in semi-public rooms lined with adjacent bedroom doors may seem a likely spot for furnishings, but often they must remain vacant to ensure a clear path to the exit door. Analysis of the actual placement of the furniture in relation to code compliance is important to ensure the design is successful.

Some theories support giving bedrooms direct access to living spaces because visual connection cues help residents to leave their room and engage in community life. The authors believe that the feeling of home trumps this theory. Direct access of bedrooms to community living areas not only reduces privacy, it changes the character of a homey living room to a "common space." The cues for engagement should be cultural; smells of kitchen, laughter from the other rooms, and the simple knowing of the household rhythms that comes with being part of home.

Placing bedrooms and bathing areas down a short bedroom hallway beyond social spaces is consistent with our personal home designs. Although governmental regulations mandate minimum hall width, the

"The bedroom hall is designed to create a buffer of privacy. In traditional nursing homes, its purpose has evolved to be a traffic way."

size of the opening to the hallway may be slightly reduced to signal a transition to more quiet private spaces beyond.

Bedrooms for residents should provide space designed to be personalized. Encourage residents and family members to bring furniture, art and other belongings to create an intimate personal space. We also suggest you avoid buying the same headboard, side table and chair style for every room. Some vendors advertise, "Create a consistent look in *your* facility," and promote purchasing everything the same. This is an institutional approach. Regulations require the organization to provide bedside tables, but nothing says they all have to be the same. And nothing says residents can't bring their own furnishings and opt not to use those provided.

Preferably all bedrooms are private, but if some rooms must be shared, the design should provide distinct physical separation between the two residents. Depending upon the size of the room, there are very creative options for making a semi-private room more private.

If each bedroom has a bathroom and shower, residents don't need to leave their private space to attend to private needs. But if each household can provide only a central bathing room, it should be located near the bedrooms. While ideally it should be possible to go to the bathing room without being seen from the public side of the household, the bathing room should have adequate space for dressing and undressing. Centralized bathing rooms should be like a health spa – a destination point where those receiving the service feel a sense of luxury and relaxation rather than the institutional "dip and spray." Spa rooms also are great places to put a beautician station.

Storage

Storage in the households should be carefully planned. Think about the items flowing into the house that must be stored until used. Storage identified for specific items should be integrated throughout the household. Linens consume a large part of a household's storage needs. If designed appropriately, bedroom closets can provide storage for sheets and towels. Additional clean linens for restocking should have central storage points. Storage along hallways provides convenient access to linens for staff and residents.

Lift equipment and other assistive devices are important for resident mobility and staff safety, but should not clutter living spaces or hallways. Niches should be planned to provide quick storage and retrieval of these devices. (Overhead track systems are one option that some find desirable.)

"Encourage residents and family members to bring furniture, art and other belongings to create an intimate personal space."

"Centralized bathing rooms should be like a health spa – a destination point of luxury and relaxation rather than the institutional 'dip and spray.'"

Households need storage for important items related to home life. Games, holiday decorations, candlesticks, the good china, books and keepsakes all may be strategically and attractively stored in rooms where they are typically used.

Medications ideally should be kept in a locked cabinet in each resident's room. Med-carts are no longer necessary. Medications that require double locking can be kept in the staff room or in an interior locked space within each resident's medicine cabinet. Check with your state survey agency in advance to be sure you have designed an approach that will pass inspection.

Utility Spaces

Appropriate design of utility spaces is critical. Access to the soiled utility room should be direct and convenient so linen and clothing bins never sit in the open. While some organizations may choose to send soiled linens and clothing in bulk to a central laundry, we suggest as much laundry as possible be done within the household.

In some states this may require two sets of washers and dryers separated for soiled and non soiled items. Household residents may choose to help with table linens or assist in washing personal clothing. Because soiled laundry must be kept apart from other washables, a separate non soiled laundry complete with folding tables and hanging rods within reach of wheelchairs should be accessible for residents who enjoy participating. Clean utility areas may possibly be integrated with laundry rooms, but ideally, a laundry room will be only a laundry room.

Staff Work Spaces

Appropriate design of work areas is vital to household staff effectiveness. Staff work areas need to be integrated into the life of the house without diminishing the feeling of home and normalcy. Roll-top desks, armoires, nooks and wireless laptops all help integrate home and service. Spaces in the households should carefully integrate design features that allow staff to be close to and part of the daily life of the house. Imagine an environment quiet and calm enough for work and home life to co-exist. Done well, the scale of the space reflects the true atmosphere of home versus the chaos of the institutional model.

Privacy requirements mandated by the federal government can be achieved through a variety of means within households. The goal is to have residents and staff together as much as possible. However, an enclosed private room must be available for conveying information that needs to be communicated over the phone (or that can be inadvertently transmitted to

"Staff work space needs to be integrated into the life of the house."

others). Making the space small allows staff to complete tasks quickly and then return to the rhythm of the house.

Garage - Shipping/Receiving

A receiving point where supplies can be properly inventoried and sorted should be designated within the household. Cabinetry strategically located can be designed to house many items in an unobtrusive and non-institutional manner. Our home garage is another place where we put big stuff we need, but don't want cluttering the house. Although it adds expense in square footage, a garage could be added to each household whether you retrofit or go with new construction. One side can be used for parking or pulling in the household car, allowing residents access to a vehicle protected from inclement weather. The other side can be used for storage, shipping, receiving and maintenance.

The Yard

Homes typically have both a front and backyard. The front of the house is where we connect to neighborhood and street activities. Front porches are nice places to sit and enjoy the day and passersby. The backyard, on the other hand, is like an outdoor living room; a semi-public social space where we invite guests, enjoy household gatherings or private moments under the blue sky. Therefore, access to both the front and backyard should be through a public side of the house and not the bedroom hallway. Doorways to the yard are great opportunities, as are well-placed windows, for bringing the outside in and creating a strong interconnection between "in" and "out."

There should be stimulating amenities in the back yard like gardens residents can work in and patios for barbequing or simply sitting in the sun. Garden pots, outdoor furniture and light posts are a few of the features that make outdoor living inviting. Storage areas for lawn, garden and patio equipment should be considered. A sand box or other children's amenities can encourage residents' grandchildren and community youth to visit and become more engaged in the life of the household.

Therapy

Depending upon your operational variables, space for therapy services may or may not need to be built into your household design. Regardless of the need for a therapy room, there should be a shift in thinking from "therapy in the therapy room only" to integrating therapy into the house where possible.

Configuring and Assembling Your Project Development Team

Now that you have strongly anchored indicators of project feasibility, a decision has been made to retrofit or build, and a clear sense of the design framework you prefer is established, you are prepared to formally assemble your development team. Some projects may be of a size and scope that warrant a developer. We assume herein that will not be the case unless you are going to convert or build a large number of households, or if your household plans are within a larger expansion project in a Full Service Retirement Community (FSRC).

If, however, you do need a development firm, it will coordinate the development team. If your project is not large enough to warrant a full-blown developer, a less expensive possibility is to hire a development coordinator who specializes in smaller undertakings. If you do not engage a developer, the owner must ensure solid development team coordination. Professionals you need to consider as part of your team include:

- **Architects and other design professionals** to plan the physical retrofit or new construction. Project engineers are brought in as subcontractors of the architect.

- **A financial feasibility consultant** to keep up with cost forecasts as the design process moves forward (you may have internal expertise). To formalize your pre-feasibility forecast, your lender/underwriter may require you to have a financial feasibility consultant.

- **A Market/demographic consultant(s)** may be required to formalize your prefeasibility market study before your lender/underwriter agrees to finance the project.

- **A marketing firm** can help you communicate your message. Often this is overlooked as part of a nursing home project, but it can be important in attracting the community to your new vision and lifestyle. This may be the same firm that does your market/demographic work.

- **A Household Model consultant** during the design and development stage of your project can simultaneously assist with the organizational and environmental design elements. They may also be able to furnish specialized operating consultants well versed in the Household Model (i.e. dining services, nursing, administrative, etc.)

- **A dining services consultant** may be desirable because of significant changes (to the degree you determine) from preparing, serving and consuming food the old centralized way to doing it in the household kitchen. The decentralized approach has major design implications for the household and may require outside assistance. (Note: Kitchen operations

"Now that you have strongly anchored indicators of project feasibility, a decision has been made to retrofit or build, and a clear sense of the design framework you prefer is established, you are prepared to formally assemble your development team."

also have organizational implications that may require outside help to train large groups of staff about food preparation, storage and sanitation safety requirements and procedures.) It is extremely important the dining services consultant has experience with the Household Model. Though the long-term care food industry is beginning to make strides, it still is entrenched in the old system. Seeking out a progressive consultant with household experience is time well spent.

- **An underwriter/lender.** Formally, your source of funds may come into the picture later in the development process depending on whether you are gathering investment capital or structuring debt as your source of capital. Either way, it is best to identify and engage the source of funds from the outset of the project. Once your pre-feasibility work reveals your project is viable, it is good to share the information with the funding source and ensure they agree with your conclusions. Building the relationship early increases their involvement and understanding of the project.

- **A general contractor** to actually build the project needs to be selected. Depending on your project's scope and team strategy, you may elect to bring on a general contractor during the initial design and planning, or choose to wait until the construction documents are complete and available for competitive bidding.

Experience Is Essential

Whatever development team configuration fits your project, we recommend all participants either have experience with the Household Model or that they become fully educated in its implications. Insist that your development team make site visits, attend workshops or engage consulting assistance to achieve that understanding.

Engaging Financial/Market Feasibility Firms

Retaining a financial/operational consultant and/or a financial modeler or CPA specializing in long-term care is very important. The former must understand long-term care operating and financial models and the latter should have forecasting experience with Household Models. Your audit firm can either provide these services or point you in the right direction. Possibly, the same entity doing your pre-feasibility work can continue throughout the project.

Whether remodeling or building new, you should ensure financial forecasts are updated as the project unfolds and projected costs change.

"Experience is essential."

"Whether remodeling or building new, you should ensure financial forecasts are updated as the project unfolds and projected costs change."

This is an important but often overlooked aspect that is key to good project management. Failure to adequately track costs can quickly put a project in the red and cause financial struggles years after it is completed. Some firms have developed interactive forecasting where changes can be made from a distance while viewing a computer screen. This can drive down onsite service costs.

Depending upon the scope of the project and the type of financing and debt structure used, you may be required to obtain formal financial and market feasibility studies. The scenarios grounded by your pre-feasibility analysis lay the foundation for the formal financial feasibility study and will establish your project's parameters. If your pre-feasibility forecast is thorough and kept current throughout the design process, you should be able to secure a formal feasibility analysis at a significantly discounted cost.

The market analysis completed during your pre-feasibility inquiry may satisfy the formal feasibility requirement depending upon its depth and how much time has lapsed. If you have additional, related requirements, they probably are limited in scope and therefore less expensive than had you not performed pre-feasibility analysis.

Determining Financing Alternatives

Each organization must evaluate which funding sources are most appropriate for their particular transformation. These may range from conventional financing, investment capital to tax-exempt or taxable revenue bonds, and fundraising (if you are a not-for-profit) or a combination thereof.

Having only limited cash at the onset not only may aggravate scarcity thinking, but also can be a very real hurdle to launching the project. You will want to analyze your ability to secure additional debt based on current operational performance and project feasibility. If in your pre-project operation you have even a small ability to increase debt, you may want to consider taking out a temporary line of credit from a local bank (or a consortium of local/regional banks.) Doing so on the front end of your efforts may preserve your existing cash while enabling you to forge ahead with development plans. The line of credit and the dollars accessed against it can usually be included in the final financing of the project. You can then pay off the line of credit at the time of actual project financing.

In addition, predevelopment and development costs are capitalized (assuming the project is eventually built) and therefore do not negatively impact your income statement. Depreciation does not begin until the project is complete and put into service – a fact unknown by many administrators. Not only do these costs not "hit" your income statement, they can be included in the total cost of the project you are financing. (This of course assumes you are financing. Some organizations are able to pay cash, have investors or raise needed funds.)

Balancing the existing operation with the vision of the future may be challenging if current operating financials and cash on hand are not robust – perhaps due to staffing, supply and debt costs along with low interest income and declining census. If this is the case, you must effectively communicate to your source of funds that you are creating a new product that you believe will attract an expanded market. Forecasting under such circumstances is very difficult, even scary, if you're accustomed to running under capacity. But as previously noted, you will likely attract new residents and revenue with a more desirable environment and lifestyle.

This illustrates, once again, the importance of a thorough pre-feasibility analysis. It may be the basis, certainly, for interim line-of-credit financing if needed. The pre-feasibility study (and later if needed, your formal feasibility study) contains the market analysis that reflects professional confidence in your ability to attract additional residents. The market analysis is combined with your financial forecast, which should include potential new revenues from additional residents. This critical information is the foundation for not only the project, but also the financing.

Marketing the Household Model to Your Community

A succinct marketing strategy is necessary for clearly communicating your new vision to potential residents, and presents an opportunity to reclaim census and promote a new identity. If you engage a marketing firm, its representatives will help you articulate your message once they clearly understand the story of transformation from institution to home. The message needs to convey your new identity in every form of communication from the organization; position advertisements, radio ads, web page, telephone conversations, person-to-person interactions… everything.

There is a new story to tell and all the marketing pieces must tell it. The new message should communicate a lifestyle, not dependence. The kind nurse with caring, sympathetic eyes hovering over the helpless elder conveys the traditional model of illness. It is the approach used by almost

"You must effectively communicate to your source of funds that you are creating a new product that you believe will attract an expanded market."

every nursing home in America. The community should connect with your new image that actively depicts a good life being fully lived.

One Household Model organization aired a television commercial showing elders drag racing with their electric carts. Another culture change organization has a video of elders scaling trees. Another highlights romance. These commercials aren't just making up things; they actually happen.

Conceptual renderings made during the design process put you in a great position to take your vision beyond traditional stakeholders to the broader community. Telling the story of your organizational and cultural transformation with drawings in hand makes for a powerful message. Speak to civic organizations, churches and anybody who will listen. You may be surprised at their reactions when they hear your vision and its potential social impact. People are so thirsty for something different they likely will see your organization's contribution to the community in a new light and welcome your vision with broad appreciation. The message is one of home and life well lived.

As our friend Rose Marie Fagan of the Pioneer Network says, "It's about rampant normalcy."

Make Development Team Part of Organizational Dialogue

Architects and designers must become part of the organizational dialogue. They must be ready to revisit design issues that need rethinking as the process evolves. If they are experienced in Household Model design, they can prompt staff to continually question which habits to leave behind and what patterns of behavior to support. If not, they will struggle with what feels like lack of decisive direction from the organization.

Many architects and consultants are practiced at giving clients that for which they ask. Conversely, providers often yield to the development team's expertise with the mindset of "do it for us," as previously mentioned. In the context of the Household Model, the development team must be part of the discovery process in partnership with the organization and its stakeholders. Consequently, they become integral with the cultural process that the organization attempts to establish through high involvement and deep sense of partnership. Giving the client "what they ask for" or "doing it for them" limits success, whereas participating with all parties in high involvement discovery expands everybody's vision and will more likely result in a very successful project.

"People are so thirsty for something different they likely will see your organization's contribution to the community in a new light and welcome your vision with broad appreciation."

"Architects and designers must become part of the organizational dialogue."

"The development team must become part of the discovery process in partnership with the organization and its stakeholders."

Expose the Design Team to Diverse Users

Ask representatives of user groups for their perspective at critical points in the planning and design process. Look for people highly regarded by their peers or constituents, and not necessarily for those with position titles. Involve service providers who have expertise that comes from daily use of specific areas you are designing. Gain the customers' perspective by including residents and family members. Consider all stakeholder groups as part of the design-team and respect all input as equally important.

Given that the organization serves residents 24 hours a day, it is difficult to have high involvement from everyone on everything. So, we suggest using the following high involvement techniques during the design phase. Consider these techniques in addition to ones you already know fit your organization.

Open Meetings

Have open meetings *before* any significant decisions are made. Invite all groups affected by the proposed changes and repeat the information during differently scheduled meetings so everyone has a chance to hear it. The goal is to gain feedback from users. Initial meetings should present ideas, not solutions. Participants know when they are being *told* what will happen versus being *asked* for input on how to make it happen. After presentations of new or significant amounts of information, people need time to digest it, so allow for reflection. Sometimes, informed discussion starts a chain reaction of creative thinking that fuels new perspectives and enthusiasm for change.

Learning Circles With All Stakeholders

One of the most effective ways to develop consensus and build a strong team while designing households is to gather people into a learning circle. Sometimes you may want only folks from a specific service area in the circle. Other times you may wish to gather employees from various service areas, or perhaps stakeholders from different vantage points, like family, residents and staff. When people from different service areas hear about each other's ideas, they are better able to place their own priorities in perspective. The big picture becomes clear.

Bring stakeholders together to develop a list of changes you are considering. Discuss the ideas on the list so everyone gains a sense of the implications presented by each proposed change. Then, assemble representatives from the various service areas into a learning circle to talk

"Consider all stakeholder groups as part of the design-team and respect all input as equally important."

"When people from different service areas hear about each other's ideas, they are better able to place their own priorities in perspective. The big picture becomes clear."

about the importance of each potential change in relation to their jobs.

Post Information and Elicit Comments

Informal conversation, open forum meetings and learning circles will lead to design images that incorporate the participants' ideas. Post the images in a place where people can study them and comment. Since many people have difficulty reading floor plans, it's good to provide additional narration or images explaining the proposed changes and design ideas. When possible, show more than one potential solution to an issue and ask for stakeholders' feedback and preferences. The final solution may be a combination of ideas from users whose suggestions were not initially considered.

Group Site Visit

Some people have difficulty conceptualizing what *can* be if they are unfamiliar with or can't see it. Often, they have to experience it before they can truly understand or value it. So, it is a great idea to do a site visit to a Household Model organization to focus on physical design. Take the architect and other development team members with you. The shared experience will energize the co-creation process.

When you visit other Household Models do not to assume "if only you had that building" it would be easy. Each design must reflect the sensitivities of the people who will live and work there and their specific sense of community identity with the place. While features of Household Models you visit may reveal potentials for your own facility, resist the temptation to ask for "one of those designs" thinking it will save you time and money in planning.

We believe each organization must create its own local expression of the Household Model based on the fundamental principles offered in this book and other guiding resources, rather than on a prescriptive approach. Cookie cutter designs risk producing a building and culture residents and staff don't fully relate to. Though well intended, such designs may be superficial and not indigenous to the local culture. The Household Model is not a franchise approach, but a framework of principles and methodologies designed to foster your own unique version that reflects your community.

"We believe each organization must create its own local expression of the Household Model based on the fundamental principles offered in this book and other guiding resources, rather than on a prescriptive approach."

"The Household Model is not a franchise approach, but a framework of principles and methodologies designed to foster your own unique version that reflects your community."

Engaging the Design Team

There are a literally hundreds of design firms that could be a part of your project. Deciding how to hire the best team depends on several variables including the scope of your project and the local professional resources available. One of the first things you can do is ask colleagues who have undertaken similar projects. Be careful, though, to clarify that you're not seeking a cookie cutter approach to change.

There may be local or regional professionals you've worked with in the past who know your organization and local code officials and have good relationships with others in the community. But if they have not worked on Household Model projects, it is all the more important you also hire a Household Model consultant to assist in the planning process.

You may want to consider a national firm. Periodicals are filled with reports of health care projects designed by such firms. Some are developing expertise in the Household Model and can help bring together all the dimensions of home in your new design. If you go local then a national firm architect with background in the Household Model may need to be on the local team.

You may want to request information on qualifications and references from two or three firms. Call their references, or perhaps a few of their clients not listed as references. This will provide an honest client perspective of the firm's qualifications and indicate whether it is easy to work with them. You can ask firms to prepare a proposal explaining how they would put the design team together and approach your specific project.

Interviews are helpful in determining which team is right for your project and how personalities will mesh. Important considerations in making a final determination are:

- The size of the firm and how long it has been in practice.
- Its experience and special expertise with Household Model projects.
- The firm's management skills and ability to work within budget/time schedules.
- Knowledge of local and state building codes, zoning and federal regulations that apply to your project.
- Experience with local code and regulatory officials.
- Interviews with people who will work on your project or with whom you otherwise will be dealing.
- Design quality and technical competence.

You should look for a design team who:

- is responsive to your needs.
- listens carefully.
- understands your organization or at least asks the right questions.
- makes you feel comfortable and with whom you have a chemistry.

Invite Your Architect to Stay the Night

Invite your architects to reside for at least twenty-four hours in your current facility. If you have semi-private rooms, pair them with roommates they are meeting for the first time. Set extra trays for them in the dining room so they can eat with all the residents. If possible, fit them into the schedule to receive a bath in your tub or shower room. The experience will sharpen their vision.

Identify and Be Clear About Goals for Change

Without a clear reason for change, design decisions will seem arbitrary to organizational stakeholders. If everyone shares a similar vision for improvements, it is easier to determine what changes should have priority over others. Use the Essential Elements (Chapter Four) and *Anatomy of a Household* and *Household Design Principles* (earlier in this chapter) to help establish goals and guide change. Engaging users in the very beginning of a design project will spur all stakeholders to take ownership and may also reveal problems that need addressing. This is a great way to get everyone on board and may uncover areas of reluctance to change.

However, you must not overly involve the daily operating staff to the point of taking your eyes off the ball. We are building the future, but not at the expense of today. The staff must know what is going on and help design the new household, but their primary responsibility is to continue providing high quality service amidst the whirlwind of development. Not only do you want to avoid quality of service issues during development, you also want to avoid census decline. Otherwise, your financial feasibility also will decline and jeopardize completing the project. Developing new buildings is vastly different than maintaining daily operations. Both must simultaneously be done well. Finding balance is not easy, but essential.

"Invite your architects to reside for at least twenty-four hours in your current facility. The experience will sharpen their vision."

"You must not overly involve the daily operating staff to the point of taking your eyes off the ball. We are building the future, but not at the expense of today."

Design Process Flushes Out Lingering Resistance or Lack of Clarity

When you start designing households, you likely will discover where resistance to change and lack of clarity still lurk within the organization. To enable the design team to help translate your vision into physical dimensions and space relationships, you need to communicate how you imagine life taking shape in the Household Model. This is where discrepancies between desired goals and resistors to change rise to the surface.

As with any transformation, there may be lingering resistance to specific changes in the physical environment. This provides a window into the mindsets of participating stakeholders. Though most may by now be behind the overall concept, some might not understand how the decentralized, "small is better" design will allow them to get their work done. Some still believe assembly line methodologies are surely most efficient. They may think assembling food trays in a central kitchen *must* be faster than making food to order in the household kitchen and wonder, "How will we be able to get it all done?!"

As leaders, we know a full understanding of change doesn't come in one gust of wind. We may be able to internalize the grand philosophy of creating home and resident-directed service and make it our own. Most of us, however, discover the full implications of deep change only in increments, sometimes one situation at a time.

For example, imagine a nurse who is excited about resident-directed service and changing the physical environment as advocated in the Household Model. He may envision his own mother moving into one of the houses and finds comfort knowing things will be different for her. The nurse may even be a powerful force in the organizational change process and eagerly interact with the design team. This same nurse, however, may be a product of traditional training and professional indoctrination. As one highly trained and qualified to provide skilled nursing care, his perspective on equipping resident rooms is unwittingly limited to the old way of doing things. He may adamantly oppose the notion of placing a medicine cabinet in each resident's room because he is convinced distribution is most efficient from a centralized med cart. Also, he makes a passionate case that decentralized distribution will result in more medication errors. Of course, the decentralized approach has proven to work very well while protecting residents' privacy, but it is not yet within the experience of this nurse.

Or think of the activities staff. They want to keep their large activity closet to store seasonal decorations, and dedicated wall space to put up a large bulletin board for announcements. Obviously, they have not yet fully absorbed the implications change holds for them.

Both professionals have yet to translate in their minds how they can provide their particular service in a normal home environment instead of in an institution. Ironically, workers commonly see how areas around them will change – we have seen it many times – but it doesn't dawn on them how their own little corner of the world will also change. It is easier to see the need to change in others than to see it in ourselves.

Initiating Leaders Must Create a Discovery Environment

The design process is a great time for formal leaders to challenge assumptions and an opportunity to stimulate conversations among stakeholders about how a true home looks and functions. The physical environment's influence on operations will help you finally flesh out what to leave behind and what new features to introduce. The ultimate physical design reflects the organization's clarity of vision, and lack thereof. Consequently, much care must be taken to fully articulate and integrate the design of the building and organizational culture. The initiating leader(s) is responsible for creating a learning environment so participants, though excited by the future they are creating, do not limit possibilities due to past frames of reference. Most importantly, the initiating leaders must self-monitor to ensure that they, too, discard what doesn't work and totally embrace the future. Whether or not leaders fully understand it, their ceiling will be by default the organization's ceiling.

Throughout the change process, an evolution of understanding, agreement and decision-making must occur for all stakeholders. This is a chance for coaching and interactive dialogue among leaders, staff, residents and the project design team (architect, interior designer and financial and marketing advisors).

"It is easier to see the need to change in others than to see it in ourselves."

"The initiating leader is responsible for creating a learning environment. Whether or not leaders fully understand it, their ceiling will be by default the organzation's ceiling."

Regulations Affect Building Design

Almost every type of building must comply with a set of regulations. These are primarily safety standards that protect the occupants and emergency response personnel who come to their aid.

They also address the occupants' expectations and patterns of behavior. As expectations and behaviors evolve, regulations addressing environmental issues may also need to evolve. A substantial time lag can occur between recognizing the evolution of behavioral patterns and modifying environmental regulations accordingly. Environments for frail adults provide a diversity of challenges as we strive to keep them safe without becoming so over-protective we deprive their lives of purpose and meaning.

Because nursing homes are now based on a medical model, most regulations address standards of care that are clinical in nature. Regulations do not inhibit the Household Model, although interpretations in some states can make it more difficult than in others.

The Fire Code is the greatest regulatory challenge to the Household Model. Its single focus is fire safety, as it must be. The problem is that local, state and federal fire marshal offices don't always use the same code. The local office may use one issued in a particular year, the state another year, and the federal yet another. While approval for your plans may be granted, brace yourself for the first fire inspector "walk through" after the building is complete.

It can be as if plan approvals never took place and the price tag can be startling. Annual inspections may bring up new issues with long-standing situations never before identified as problems. Fire Marshal inspections are one of the regulatory system's most expensive for providers. Another fire code reality is that nobody outside its bureaucracy seems to know how to interact with, influence or penetrate it. So, it is a reality we must live with. Having an architect familiar with the code will save you much heartache. Stories of woe over fire codes frequently involve architectural issues that a knowledgeable architect can help you avoid.

ENVIRONMENTAL
The Debate Begins
Alignment of Vision
Engage Partners in Design
Move In
Home

MOVE IN

Planning Move-In

Don't underestimate the need to plan and prepare for the physical move into your new households. Once you've developed design drawings clearly identifying all rooms and spaces for furniture, start planning the upcoming move. Time frames and schedules for moving must be determined so clinicians and others can plan ahead to assure resident safety and wellbeing.

You may want to create an ad hoc transition team responsible for high involvement planning of the logistics and variables necessary to ensure a smooth move into the households. You need to bring all your project management skills to bear with this team. A project checklist, frequent stand-up meetings, high involvement across the organization and lots of communication are very important.

"You may want to create an ad hoc transition team responsible for high involvement planning of the logistics and variables necessary to ensure a smooth move into the households."

A facility was living the Household Model in their original building while new households were being built. Once the new facility was completed, a group of managers, trying to be helpful, went to the new facility to set up the households with supplies. Putting linens in closets, utensils and tools in kitchen cupboards, etc. For six months after moving day household staff was still struggling to find stuff. Moral of the story: those who thought they were helping out by setting everything up in advance realized that those who worked in the household really *do* need to be involved in every aspect of change and transformation.

As the design process evolves from schematics to construction documents, financing and construction will be prominent in your life until time to move is just around the corner. This period brings growing excitement, fear and anticipation. The moment everybody has been waiting for is almost here!

While the construction and insurance people won't get too excited about it, residents and staff will be eager for a peek at the new place. A hardhat tour with small groups of residents and staff may be possible if you communicate with your insurer and take all necessary precautions to guarantee the site is safe and supervised by construction and operating personnel. A tour will raise the excitement level to new heights. People will finally see where they will live and work. The closer to moving day, the more excitement there is.

But there also can be fear if the transition is not well planned so people know their place in it all: Which house will I live in? Who will I live by? Who will work in my house? Which house will I work in? Who will I work with?

Letting these questions go unanswered for too long breeds fear. "Not knowing" is part of the change process, but as time draws near lingering uncertainty can be unhealthy. People need to know and help direct their circumstances.

Some Household Model organizations take this process very seriously and go to great lengths to ensure existing personal relationships determine where people live and work. There is really no other way truly consistent with the Household Model. After all, this is about creating home, and home is where we live with people we love.

We in long term care are so used to making decisions based on institutional criteria, it is counterintuitive for us to believe we can actually "let" people live and work with those they love and still cover all the operational bases. We were no different at Meadowlark Hills. We did the first several months of planning for transition into households in 2001 with the idea we would place residents in specific houses based on their level of care.

In retrospect, we're embarrassed to admit we spent so much time organizing around that assumption. But it made perfect sense at the time that level one people should be in one house, level two in the next and so on. We got so smart about it we figured we could staff lighter in level one and higher in the level four house. It made perfect sense. It took quite awhile to dawn on us it not only was a bad approach operationally, it was not even close to being resident-directed or even resident-centered.

For one thing, as we planned placement of each resident we realized their individual situations change frequently. At each planning meeting there would invariably be a team report like, "Mrs. Smith is now a level three instead of two." Then the group would spend time reshuffling the placement lineup. After several months of this, somebody finally asked, "Is this how it is going to work? Every time somebody switches levels they move to another house?"

This spawned other questions. "Are people going to live in fear that every time they have a new set of needs they have to move?" and "I thought we were trying to create home; this doesn't sound like home to me!"

We were thinking in a box without any new ideas for initial resident "placement." Our thought process seemed perfectly logical in the healthcare world.

Finally somebody said, "Why don't we arrange people based on who they want to live by?"

Well, that seemed completely impractical! How could it possibly work? But in absence of a better idea, we decided to survey residents about whom they would like for neighbors. The idea graduated to also asking residents who they preferred working in their house. It further evolved to asking staff which residents they felt close to and would like to serve. And finally, which coworkers would you like on your team?

After receiving survey responses from residents and staff, we began piecing the puzzle together, using relationships as the primary factor in determining staff and resident placement in the new households. It worked. In fact, it was much easier – and far more satisfying – to organize than before. People were able to live and work with whom they preferred. We also discovered the need to have a full compendium of staff (RN, LPN,

Aides, etc.) in each house was not at odds with the relationship-based approach.

The experience taught us we must put the person first and set aside institutional thinking, and that relationships can and should drive the journey.

It is scary to realize the impact conventional leadership thought processes and assumptions have on groups of people. What if nobody had challenged placing residents in households based on levels of care!? It dawned on us our job was not to place residents, but help elders establish their homes on their own terms.

Individualize Each Resident's Move In

Once it is determined where residents will live, individualize their move. Help them decide how to arrange their room and where to put their personal possessions by giving each a room plan and sitting down with them and any family members they wish to include. What they decide can be an individualized installation plan to guide the movers. Then, when residents move into their new homes, everything will be as they envisioned.

We recommend you emphasize to residents and families the importance of bringing residents' personal belongings. Often, family members consider dispersing the loved one's belongings before moving the elder to a nursing home. Encourage them instead to bring meaningful artifacts to help complete the elder's new home.

When financing is in place, ground is broken and move-in plans have been developed, there will be mixed emotions of excitement and fear. Build on this shared passion to make it all come together. It's amazing what can be accomplished when everybody is aligned around a common vision and purpose. Take note of the magic. It will be all around you.

When time comes to move, it feels just like moving into a new house...because it is. It takes a few weeks to notice households establishing their own rhythms. But they will.

It All Comes Together

By now the self-led teams are in operation. Their vision, day-to-day workings and attitudes will support the new home and vice versa. The residents and the self-led teams are building relationships that will help all involved through the transition. Individual, leadership, organizational and

"It dawned on us our job was not to place residents, but help elders establish their homes on their own terms."

"We recommend you emphasize to residents and families the importance of bringing residents' personal belongings."

"It's amazing what can be accomplished when everybody is aligned around a common vision and purpose. Take note of the magic. It will be all around you."

environmental transformations are solidly integrated. *This* is what you have been working for. Together, strong and proud, you evict institutionalism from your home and lives.

One Household Model organization decided they really needed to mark the transition from old to new so they decided to have a bonfire with staff and residents. They burned a piece of the old nurses' station, a bib, a restraint – anything they could find that represented "the old way." Residents were encouraged to write down things they didn't like about the old way-things-were-done and burn those papers too. With the bonfire they were about to cross over a line and begin anew the next day.

ENVIRONMENTAL

The Debate Begins

Alignment of Vision

Engage Partners in Design

Move In

Home

YOU ARE HOME

And so, here you are. Everyone can now enjoy the fruits of all your hard work: a sense of family, purpose and belonging is felt by all who live and work in the household. It's extraordinary, isn't it?

However, to sustain the good work you have done the organization must stay committed to the Essential Elements of the Household Model.

Begin With Ritual

We mark significant events in our lives – from birthdays, marriage, graduation and holidays to death – with rituals. Whether formal or not, each ritual is sacred in its own right.

Moving into a new home, and especially moving from a conventional nursing home into a Household Model, is a significant event. Some cultures have rituals to bless a new home or "warm" a house. The following is a house blessing conducted by Meadowlark Hills when opening of the houses occured. The blessing was followed by a housewarming with shared food, conversation, song and laughter. This particular house blessing ceremony is adapted with permission from Father Edward Hayes' house blessing ritual in his prayer book, "Prayers for the Domestic Church."

Part One

Celebrant: Father, our God, you whose home is in heaven, on earth, and in that undiscovered beyond, come and bless this house which is now to be our home. Surround this shelter with your Holy Spirit. Encompass all it's four sides with the power of your protection so that no evil or harm will come near.

May that divine blessing shield this home from destruction, storm, sickness and all that might bring evil to us who shall live and work within these walls.

(A moment of silence, the celebrant sprinkles water on the front door)

Blessed be this doorway. May all who come to it be treated with respect and kindness. May all our comings and goings be under the seal of God's loving care. Blessed be all the rooms of this home,

(name of household). May each of them be holy and filled with the spirit of happiness. May no dark powers ever be given shelter within any of these rooms but banished as soon as recognized.

(Light a candle located on the table with the bread, wine and salt)

Blessed be this living room may we truly live within it as people of peace. May prayer and playfulness never be strangers within its walls.

(Turn toward the dining room/kitchen)

Blessed be this place where we shall eat. May all our meals be sacraments of the presence of God as we are nourished at these alter-tables. Blessed be the shrine of the kitchen. Blessed be the herbs and spices, and the pots and pans used to prepare our meals. May the ill-seasonings of anger and bitterness never poison the meals prepared here.

(Turn toward hall archways leading toward bedrooms)

Blessed be these bedrooms. Here we shall find rest, refreshment and renewal. May the spirits of love and affection, together with the spirits of angelic care, touch all who shall use these rooms.

(Turn back toward living room)

Let us pause now and pray in silence as each of us calls down the holy blessing of God upon this house – now become our home.

(Pause for silent prayer)

Resident: Lord our God, may your divine name be always holy within our home.

May you, as Holy Father and Divine Mother, secure loving care for all who shall live and work here.

May your Kingdom come in this home as we love and respect one another. May we always do your holy will by living and working in harmony and unity.

Family Member: May we never suffer from lack of bread, nor from a lack of all that we need to nourish our family. May the spirit of pardon and forgiveness reside with us and be always ready to heal our divisions. May the spirits of mirth and laughter, hope and faith, playfulness and prayer, compassion and love be perpetual guests in our home.

Staff Member: May our door be always open to those in need. Open be this door to the neighbor or to the stranger. May our friends who come to us in times of trouble and sorrow, find our door open to them and to their needs. May the holy light of God's presence shine forth brightly in this home and be a blessing for all who shall live and work here and for everyone who shall come to this door.

Celebrant: May God's holy blessing rest upon us all.

Part Two

(All turn their attention to the table/alter where an unlit candle, the wine, bread and salt are arranged on the table.)

Celebrant: We offer gifts for this house in celebration of our shared beginning.

Resident (Holding up the Bread): Bread…that this house may never know hunger.

Family Member (Holding up the Salt): Salt…that life may always have flavor.

Staff Member (Holding up the Wine): Wine…that joy and prosperity may reign forever.

Celebrant: We give and receive these gifts with great wonder and thankfulness for our many blessings.

Part Three

Celebrant: We are here to dedicate Honstead House. May our actions today receive the blessings of God, and may the purposes and dreams, which have brought us to this point of beginning, be fulfilled.

People: We dedicate ourselves toward helping this house embody all that it is meant to be. We commit ourselves to uphold our responsibilities in making this house a home of joy and laughter, of thoughtfulness, caring, and shared living between residents, staff, family, friends and community. We further dedicate to uphold our responsibilities in making this house a symbol of what can be in store for others across this nation who wish to follow.

Celebrant: Then upon you, the residents, family, staff, friends and community, is the obligation to be supportive and steadfast in creating the culture of this house that will symbolize the commitment and beliefs that have brought it into being.

People: We dedicate this house today.

Celebrant: That this house will be a place of nourishment, joy, fulfillment of dreams and peace.

People: We dedicate this house today.

Celebrant: That the lifestyle in this house will be seed for growth across this land in changing the lives of our elders, that a new standard will become the hallmark of this place, in our town, state and nation.

People: We dedicate this house today.

All: May God bless our efforts on behalf of this house.

Blessing the new home is the first of many ceremonies and celebrations residents will experience in the Household Model. Each of you who have embarked upon this deep journey of transformation will be blessed as well. You will be an instrument of liberation for elders and of change in the character of your community. The painful unlearning and the joyous discoveries along your journey will enrich you forever.

Blessings upon you and your household.

Epilogue

Michael

I had just come home from my friend Michael's memorial service. When we first began discussing the Household Model and what that could mean for the elders, I was on board. Closer, more intimate relationships would enable us to better know our elders' needs and desires. But I had no idea what this would mean for one man who would struggle and lose a battle with early onset Alzheimer's disease.

Michael moved into our household almost two years ago. He had known his diagnosis for about eight years, but as the disease progressed he became less able to name his foe. He told me, "I have Alzheimer's and it makes me so infuriated!"

Michael's fury stemmed, in part I suspect, from his nature. He was a retired philosophy professor at the local university and very active in his community politically and socially. He was an ACLU member, a Democrat (he was very glad to inform me) and an atheist. He loved a good fight, but this foe didn't fight fair.

I didn't anticipate developing a strong friendship, as we certainly didn't have a lot of common interests, but as the weeks passed our friendship grew. I found Michael had a very broad taste in music and I had a great appreciation for almost all of his 3,000 CDs. Michael also told me of his travels to Turkey, where he fell in love…with the bean.

Michael could drink four double espressos in one setting. Those who know Michael are nodding in agreement here. At every opportunity Michael and I would sneak off to the café for good conversation and a taste of the bean. We would talk of politics, religion, philosophy and Alzheimer's.

Michael was in charge of Michael's life. Just because he had a disease didn't mean he didn't have the power to make decisions. Michael chose to hire companions who could ride a bicycle with him and take him to the café and to local hangouts to listen to live music. He also chose to fire companions. He let one fellow go for criticizing Messiaen, his favorite French composer. I asked if this was the only reason for letting him go, and Michael confided that the "oaf" also felt reading the dictionary was a waste of time. From that day forward I informed the new companions that listening to music was one of Michael's favorite pastimes and it probably wasn't wise to criticize your boss's taste in music.

Toward the end of Michael's life we debated the benefit of employing companions for him. Not wanting to waste his family resources, I asked for others' input on when we should discontinue the practice. One team member team asked, "If they are holding his hand and playing his favorite music on his stereo, is that a waste of his resources?"

No, we decided, it probably is what Michael had in mind the whole time.

Not every companion could continue working with Michael as he declined physically. One fellow stopped when Michael began using a wheelchair. To their credit, they gave each other the freedom to part as friends.

A short time later Michael was unable to walk, and then to sit up or move independently. Through it all he continued to communicate on a primary level.

Because of our relationship I still could understand Michael. The Thursday before he died it rained a lot. I mentioned it to him and he said, very Michael-like, "That sucks."

Three days later he asked what was wrong with him. I had an honest relationship with Michael, so with love I told him he was dying. He said, "That sucks. Do I have to do it now?"

I told him I didn't know when it would happen but I could stay with him for a while if he wanted, and he nodded. Tears streamed from his eyes and mine, too. He had the benefit of a floor bed, which allowed me to lie on the floor next to him and wrap my arms around him. I stayed with him until he was soundly sleeping.

The companions also laid on the floor next to Michael. They played Messiaen, Elvis, Philip Glass and a CD of his sister playing oboe as a member of the Houston Symphony. Annie, a household team member and friend, brought a coffee maker into his room and brewed gourmet coffee to create an aroma familiar and pleasing to him.

As his respiration slowed, others dropped by to say goodbye. Each would lie next to Michael on the floor, touch and talk to him and pour out their love and best wishes.

Michael died the next day at 5:21 a.m. Workers in the house called me at home with the news. I wiped my tears and went to the kitchen to make a pot of gourmet coffee.

- Shari Brown

Bibliography

Carboni, Judith T., "Homelessness Among the Institutionalized Elderly," *The Journal of Gerontological Nursing*, Vol. 16, No. 7 (1990).

Cooper Marcus, Clare. "Self-identity and the Home." *Housing; Symbol, Structure, Site*. Cooper-Hewitt Museum, The Smithsonian Institution 1990.

Dovey, K. "Dwelling, archetype and ideology." *Center*, 8, 9-21 (1993).

Fisher, Kimball. *Leading Self-Directed Work Teams: - A Guide to Developing New Team Leadership Skills*. New York: McGraw Hill, 2000.

Fox, Nancy, LaVrene Norton, Arthur W. Rashap, Joe Angelelli, Vivian Tellis-Nyak, Mary Tellis-Nyak, Leslie A. Grant, Sandy Ransom, Susan Dean, SueEllen Beatty, Dawn Brostoski, William Thomas. "Well-Being: Beyond Quality of Life - The Metamorphosis of Eldercare." Action Pact Press (2005)

Gladwell, Malcolm. *The Tipping Point:- How Little Things Can Make Big Difference*. New York: Little, Brown and Company, 2000.

Greenleaf, Robert K. *Servant Leadership: - A Journey Into the Nature of Legitimate Power and Greatness*. Mahwah, NJ: Paulist Press, 1977.

Helmstetter, Shad. *You Can Excel In Times of Change*. New York: River Productions Inc., 1991.

His Holiness the Dalai Lama and Howard C. Cutler, M.D. *The Art of Happiness at Work*. New York: Riverhead Books, 2003.

Jacobs, Robert W. *Real Time Strategic Change:- How to Involve an Entire Organization in Fast and Far-Reaching Change*. San Francisco: Berrett-Koehler Publishers, 1994.

Kaup, M. L. "Reshaping behaviors in nursing homes by reshaping nursing home architecture: A case study in the investigation of change." *Proceedings to the Environmental Design Research Association*, USA, 34, 98-104. (2003).

Kouzes, James M. and Barry Z. Posner. *The Leadership Challenge:- How to Keep Getting extraordinary Things Done in Organizations*. San Francisco: Jossey-Bass Inc., 1995.

Land, George and Beth Jarman. *Breakpoint Change and Beyond:- Mastering the Future – Today.* Champaign, Ill.: Harper Business, 1992.

Lawrence, R. *Housing, Dwellings, and Home: design theory, research, and practice.* New York: John Wiley & Sons, 1987.

Mickus, M., Luz, C., Hogan, A., "Voices From The Front: Recruitment and Retention of Direct Care Workers in Long-Term Care Across Michigan," Michigan State University, (2004).

Norberg-Schulz, C. *The Concept of Dwelling: on the way to figurative architecture.* New York: Rizzoli International Publications, Inc., 1985.

Peters, Tom, *Design: Innovate Differentiate Communicate.* New York: Dorling Kindersley Limited, 2005.

Pink, Daniel H. *A Whole New Mind:- Moving from the Information Age to the Conceptual Age.* New York: Riverhead Books, 2005

Prochaska, James O. Ph. D., John C. Norcross, Ph. D. and Carlo C. Diclemente, Ph. D. *Changing for Good:-A Revolutionary Six-Stage Program for Overcoming Bad Habits and Moving Your Life Positively Forward.* New York: Quill, HarperCollins Publishers, Inc., 1994.

Quinn, Robert E. *Building the Bridge as You Walk On It:- A Guide for Leading Change.* San Francisco: Jossey-Bass, 2004.

Rees, Fran. *How to Lead Work Teams: Facilitation Skills*. San Diego: Pfeiffer & Company, 1991.

Schwartz, B. *Nursing Home Design: consequences for employing the medical model*. New York: Garland Publishing, 1996.

Seavey, Dorie, "The Cost of Frontline Turnover in Long-Term Care," Better Jobs, Better Care, (2004).

Senge, Peter M. *The Fifth Discipline:- The Art and Practice of the Learning Organization*. New York: Doubleday, 1990.

Watson, Gregory H. *Business Systems Engineering*. Hoboken, NJ: John Wiley & Sons, Inc., 1994

Acknowledgements

We, the authors, are a bit of a sham. We have the heart and soul. And even the magic of the inspiring word. But we were shored up on all sides in this venture by great friends and colleagues. Thanks to those who contributed to our chapters on organization and environment, Linda Bump, Migette Kaup and Jeff Anderzohn. A special thanks to Imy Higbie who contributed to Chapter 2. She thought beyond her own experience and stepped out as an activist to awaken others to the nursing home experience.

Thanks to our moonbeams from first word to last: Keith Schaeffer and Steph Kilen, both strong writers shedding quiet light on our struggles. They reworked our clumsy words and thoughts, questioned our logic, confronted assumptions, gently pressuring us to get it right. And thanks to our outstanding research assistant, Codi Thurness.

We, wish to thank the three entities who provided the leadership and funding that enabled Meadowlark Hills Retirement Community to produce it: the Sunflower Foundation of Topeka Kansas, Kansas Department on Aging and The Commonwealth Fund of New York City. They share a vision that the changes offered in this collection become widespread. Each has our gratitude and admiration.

Thanks to the Board of Directors of Meadowlark Hills for recognizing that the need to change how frail elders live in long-term care exists well beyond the Flint Hills of Kansas. It reflects their character and the community of Manhattan, Kansas.

Thank you residents of Meadowlark Hills. You have opened your home to thousands of people from nearly every state in the union and at least 17 foreign countries who have come to learn a new way to live and work. Thank you, each and every one of you, for your generous hospitality to so many. You saw the importance of this journey from the beginning and along the way encouraged all of us to keep moving forward.

Thank you to Megan Hannan, Rose Marie Fagan, Bill and Jude Thomas, Barry and Debbie Barkan, Nancy Fox, Tom Zwicker and Debbie Van Straten, Bill Keane, Sue Misiorski, Joanne Radar, Charlene Boyd, David Green, Garth Brokaw, Patricia Maben, Carter Williams, and Wendy Lustbader. Your aligned vision is surpassed only by your deep commitment and personal sacrifice on behalf of elders and staff everywhere. Your perseverance is striking the bell of truth and awakening the nation's conscience.

Thanks to those who helped review this work; Deborah Douglas, David Slack, Migette Kaup, Jeff Chapman, Martha Ann Olson, Gail Urban, Willie Novotny, Bill and Sally Boone, Marsha Blatchford, Bill Witte, Chris Keysor, Carmen Bowman, Courtney Bouker and Paul Young.

Special thanks to Meadowlark Hills residents, Elnora Young and Carol Chalmers, for your extra mile of commitment of time and wisdom during your respective reviews. You both were invaluable.

We thank the Pennybyrn at Maryfield, Wesley Retirement, Lenawee County and Perham Memorial organizations for sharing their stories in this book.

To the staff and friends at Action Pact: You helped us start our journey, and accompanied us to this day. Neither our transformation nor this Toolkit could have been done nearly so well without your partnership. Your leadership is extraordinary. Your magazine *Culture Change Now* and website of the same name have educated many world-wide. With a staff of culture change experts supported by educators, writers, artists and a great videographer, your skill set is unique and ideal. You have consistently given the field of long-term care the transformation tools it needs. Your voice has quietly, yet forcefully prodded us all to become what we are truly called to be.

Thanks to my mother and father who inspired me to commit my life to elders. My father's quiet wisdom and awareness are constant, guiding forces in my life. I feel blessed that the Household Model came in to being in time for him. My mother gave her children tenacity, courage and intolerance for social injustice. I beg her forgiveness for not seeing the injustice of her long-term care experience before she died. Her painful road became my difficult path to personal discovery.

Thank you, LaVrene. You are an amazing friend, colleague, change agent and visionary. Co-authoring a book with a friend is a little like wallpapering with your spouse. If you survive it, the relationship only grows stronger. We passed the test.

Lastly, I thank my family. The additional energy and time required to write it were, in large part, granted and supported by the home front. Thank you Sally for your understanding, patience and constant support during your own time of loss. I love you.

To our ten-year-old son, Ben, you have been a trooper during the many absences required for writing this book. You know how much I love you.

I asked Ben, a voracious reader, to review Chapter One. He got about half a page down, put it aside and said, "No dragons, no dragon slayers…it's boring Dad."

When you are older Ben, I hope you will see there *are* dragons in this book; that our only real hope for change rests with the dragon slayers who read it.

- Steve

Thank you, Meadowlark Hills staff members for your courage, heart, commitment and generosity of spirit. As individuals and part of the team, you are living examples of how societal change occurs when people align around values and vision, and commit to the required actions.

You lived the changes from the beginning, and in so doing are a testament to the industry's highest principles. If this book were a play, you would be its scriptwriters. Ultimately, the toll taken on each of you will be forgotten, but the gifts that come from leading others to a new way will endure forever.

I am so grateful for the personal inspiration of elders and staff that I have met across the US. And especially for those who took the first steps toward Households with Action Pact: Bigfork Valley, Meadowlark Hills, Nielson Place, Tealwood and Lenawee. You have proved that true home can happen in the Household Model.

A special thanks to all my friends in Australia but especially to Sarah, Peter and Dawn MacKenzie of Melbourne and Rhonda Peploe of Perth. You have welcomed me into your homes as your elders have welcomed me into their households.

Thanks Steve. You have proved The Household Model is home and sustainable. And the side benefit is that all those great conversations of ours over the years have not remained static in time – they've become a book!

I thank my family and dear friends, embedded not only in my heart, but luckily also in Action Pact. Everywhere I turn I am supported. You all have passed me by in your knowledge and skills, but find the energy to listen and counsel me and even find my lost keys. You are my inspiration and my motivation.

Thank you Pat, Brendan, Chris, Patty, Keith, Kristine, Coletta, Steph, Megan, Linda, Peggy, Deb, Mary Ellen, Mike, Paula, Andy and Michaele.

And Mike, thank you for inspiring our life plan – we'll be old together, and it will be home, wherever we happen to live.

- LaVrene